Experts
Of
Our Potential

A STORY THAT WILL CHANGE

HOW YOU DELIVER VALUE

BRIAN FRETWELL

ISBN: 197425299X
ISBN-13: 978-1974252992

DEDICATION

This book is dedicated to Jamie.

My partner and co-conspirator.

For helping me understand the connection between vulnerability, courage, and love through the gift that is our life together.

You've helped make authenticity and this book, possible for me.

I'll never be afraid to love you more

.

CONTENTS

PREFACE

You'll notice something missing in this book— and that's the experts. There is no quote by a famed PhD claiming it will change your life or a New York Times blurb calling this the most important book of the year. Instead, I wrote with a different kind of expert in mind.

I started this project nearly a decade ago, convinced I was building a how-to guide for the modern workplace. But that workplace changed faster than I could write, and I realized the book would be out of date before the ink dried. Along the way a deeper story emerged.

Truth be told, writing Experts of Our Potential wrung me inside out. I challenged absolutely everything I thought was true, and I came up against some big questions. Does modern life give us more personal freedom or less? How do we define job success when the rules change by the day? In the new economy, why do some soar and some perish?

Reaching yet deeper, what would we do if we knew exactly what we were meant to do, right now? And who is really standing in our way?

You'll find the answers in a complex friendship between a

flawed, brilliant and self-immolating worker named Chris and the consultant who tries to help him. This book shares their conversations through some of life's biggest ups and downs. In those exchanges—sometimes heated, sometimes desperate—you'll discover a bit of neuroscience, psychology, business advice, and most of all, hope.

As Chris and his coach bare their souls for us, I hope you will find answers in their honesty and permission in their courage. Most of all, I hope you find the courage to make your own story. Because you are that expert—already.

- Brian Fretwell, August 2017

1
DOUBT

I once had this client...

How many times have I wanted to tell his story?

I used to be a performance consultant; something like a professional coach for those looking to climb the business ladder. As a coach and consultant, I focused on success, on goal setting, and on very defined strategies to help my clients reach their mark. It was a successful approach.

Until Chris.

In this business, I see people at their best and their worst. I hear things nobody else hears, or should hear. I work under a non-disclosure agreement. I have never gone back to a client to see if I could actually share their information—until now.

Chris was my most difficult client. In fact, Chris was the client who got me out of the performance business altogether. So many times I struggled, despite my training, to figure out what was going on in his head. At his best, he seemed almost unstoppable. At his worst, he was uncertain and unconvincing, with a cloud of doom above his head. The challenge was figuring out which Chris would show up.

My work and my philosophy required me to believe that something more is always available. I could see something special glowing in there somewhere, that left an impression no matter if he was on top of his game or veering completely off course, again. He was the client who continuously haunted me.

Given everything we had been through, I decided to take a chance and ask his permission to tell this story. Maybe I simply caught him in a good moment, but he agreed to let me tell everything, just the way it happened. So I immediately began writing.

This book is a rare chance for me to open up about the toughest coaching I've done; perhaps my biggest failure ever. Chris opened my eyes, challenged my perception of success, and brought me to the edge right alongside him. Thanks to his story, I am able to give an honest accounting of what it's like for someone to hit bottom and where the story goes from there.

Through our frank dialogues, recounted here to the best of my ability, you will find a recurring thread: In a world that is changing and becoming less certain, how do we regain control and quiet the anxiety, keep it from becoming overwhelming, and allow our brains to operate at full capacity? How do we develop the confidence to both understand our value and do what it takes to communicate it to the world?

How deep do we have to dig to discover the real power that lies within? And once we do, can anything keep us from using it to change the world?

I'm sharing with you the client who changed me forever. As a coach, I prided myself on having the answer. But my ready answers were not what he needed. Instead, it turned out the discovery we would make together was something we would both need to move forward.

I welcome you to sit through some of our most difficult conversations, starting with one of the most challenging moments he presented as a client...

"Chris, I noticed when you came in that you were limping, is everything ok?"

He sits down abruptly. "Sure, everything is fine. Nothing like tearing my Achilles to add an exclamation point to the worst week of my life."

I almost can't bear to look at him today, with the way he wears that discouragement. He used to be my most exciting client. You could see him learning and growing by leaps and bounds. His motivation seemed limitless, and his ability to deal with adversity was amazing.

"Worst week of your life? That sounds pretty extreme, care to fill me in?" I try to keep it positive, keep it light. His underlying passion could get hold of him and limit his ability to think clearly, and I just try to help him pump the brakes.

"Sure, calm down, it's no big deal. You're just like everyone else. Trying to tell me that three major failures in four years is not that big of a deal. That I'll find other things to do. That I'm not some embarrassment, a joke in the community, that people aren't talking about me. It's just not true. I see it in their eyes, I know the discussions they're having behind my back."

"You are not a failure, Chris. You've just hit some bumps in the road. Shutting your business down happened four years ago, and you could never have predicted that dream manager position would be cut when they laid off one-third of the company."

It's always important to give a client perspective, especially when they're drowning in self-pity. Like many of my clients, Chris had been through some tough professional situations after the economic downturn of 2008. Getting him, like the others, back on track, engaged and hopeful seemed to be my full-time job. Fearful minds are hard to focus. It was especially tough with Chris.

"I just got word that the company I've been working for over the last two years is being sold," Chris says bitterly. "I won't have a job and I'm not even going to get the commission on the big account I just sold because my sale won't be final until after the buyout."

So much of the work we had done in the last couple of years was preparing him to land exactly this kind of account. After the other setbacks, this victory would be a big deal. It's not just that he had been counting on this; I had been counting on this as well. My job was to help him be successful and that sale was going to be a victory for us both.

"That's really crappy, Chris. I'm sorry to hear that." Now I settle myself down. I am upset at the situation for him on one hand, and preparing for him to question my work for him on the other.

"To top all of this off, I tore my Achilles while running this week, so I can't even go blow off steam. Running is the only thing I had felt truly successful doing in the last couple of years, and now I may never run again. It's like I can't do anything without something screwing up. Like every time I set a goal, something gets in the way. So much for being a motivational speaker. The only thing it appears I am good at is spectacular failures."

He had always taken things very personally. In many ways, it's what contributed to his ability to grow in challenging situations. But this time it was overwhelming him. As much as I tried to tell him there were things in his life that were going well, all he could see was a giant neon sign that read FAILURE.

Running was another area we were working on together. The overlapping themes of goal setting, performance improvement, and overall achievement allowed us to work on his professional goals and his running goals at the same time. Losing both his job and his defining activity simultaneously was huge.

He nearly spits out the next few words as his eyes narrow. "Look at me! Ridiculous. I'm a dream manager that can't reach his own dreams. I wanted to be a motivational speaker and now the only thing I'm motivated to do is drink a beer and crawl under the couch. My career is garbage. Who wants my advice if I can't make it work on me?"

In front of my eyes, he is becoming his very own worst enemy. His proud nature was great at gaining momentum, but that motion could go either direction.

"I don't know what to do next. I haven't told anyone what happened yet, not even my wife."

I've seen people completely break their lives apart in these moments. Once a person's mind heads down this path of destruction, it's difficult to pull back. His next steps were going to be vitally important. In fact, they could impact the rest of his life.

"Chris," I say gently, "it sounds like we need to make a couple of short-term plans here. I know it's hard, but I think we have to get something for you to work on as quickly as possible."

I know the importance of shifting his focus; of getting something small to work on so it doesn't feel like the sky is falling. But he isn't listening to me. Nothing I can say seems to have the ability to cut through the fear and anxiety.

He stares off into the distance and begins to talk in a way that sounds something like a confession.

"We were in the car yesterday when she started to ask about the vacation we were planning. It was what we were going to do with some of the proceeds from the sale, that and pay down a big part of this debt from the business that went south. I didn't even have the guts to tell her what had really happened to me.

"She was talking to me and I just went numb, I remember feeling my hands on the wheel and tightening my grip while driving down the road. As we kept talking, my hands clenched the steering wheel harder and harder. I felt like I was losing control of everything, and struggling to even keep ahold of the car.

"When we got out, I ran into the bathroom. I turned on the fan so she wouldn't hear me and began to throw up. I was shaking horribly. It was as if the anxiety was a physical thing and I was trying to get it out of my stomach.

"Security, that's what I am supposed to provide. But how can I do that when I feel so out of control?"

I sit patiently. Believing that, maybe, saying it out loud is letting him relieve some of the built-up pressure. If I can just stay with him, it might keep him from exploding and completely breaking apart. That is progress enough for today. But in his current spiral, even that was starting to seem to be too much.

"Look, I think I might be wasting my time and your time as a consultant in these sessions. You should find a client that has their shit together much more than I do, and I should quit trying to shoot for the goals that are obviously way over my head."

Instantly, my own thoughts begin to race again. If I can't help him, what does it say about me?

He continues to speak before I can get a word in. "Yesterday, I pulled out my resume. I thought, who the hell am I kidding. I've worked so hard to make this thing look good and what has it gotten me? I don't know what I want anymore but I sure know that I don't want to feel like this ever again. Maybe I'm reaching too high, maybe I just don't have what it takes, maybe this failure is just who I am."

This is excruciatingly painful to watch. This guy is a shell of who he used to be. I have seen this in my clients so many times in the turbulence of the last couple years that I know it well. Chris is fighting a battle on the inside; one that is challenging his belief in his own competence, his abilities, and his very vision of himself.

I throw out one last lifeline, hoping that I haven't lost him completely. "It's good to get it out, Chris, this is healthy. But let's not make any decisions right now. Would it be okay if we just scheduled one more appointment? I'm not ready to give up yet, and I hope you aren't either."

He hangs his head to the side and looks doubtful. "I guess. I don't know what good it will do. I suppose, if nothing else, I could at least have you help me with my resume."

That was all I needed. A breather, a little time to catch my own breath and figure out what was going on. Had it been just Chris going through this turmoil, I would have doubled down on our strategies and helped him find the next position. But something was changing in the market. Something I had seen it in too many clients and I needed some time to figure out. In order to help my clients gain a sense of self-control, I would have to consider challenging my own strategies and testing my own assumptions.

In this business, I've learned a simple truth: fate is imagination made real when a person believes the prophecy formed in their nightmares. Now my client was believing his worst. So many of the things we used to be able to count on in our professional lives had changed, not just in 2008 but before and certainly after.

What neither of us knew is that this conversation, and the ones to follow, were part of a much larger transition, something that nearly everyone was, and still is, learning to deal with personally and professionally. The things he was taking so personally were simply micro events in something that was happening on a macro scale.

The security we used to count on seemed to be lost. The strategies we traditionally relied on and the paths we followed were changing. Chris had just lost his job and now his running, which he was deeply passionate about, without any warning. Everything that seemed to provide him direction, gone in a moment. But that was simply a pebble in a landslide that was catching millions of people, including me, by surprise.

While I didn't know it at the time, this would be my last day as a performance consultant.

2
EDUCO

"I'm going to be a motivational speaker."

I still remember very clearly the day Chris said it. Back then, he was fired up, hopeful and full of life. He had initially sought coaching to help figure out what he would do once he completed his MBA. Now, it seemed, he was starting to create some real plans.

It all started back in 2004, four years before his torn Achilles and shredded dreams. The spark was a simple compliment he received after delivering the best man's speech at a wedding. Chris had prepared for weeks for the toast, rewriting his speech multiple times and bringing note cards in his suit pocket. While he knew his entire hometown would be present, given his friend's father was a prominent businessman, the only thing he cared about was getting the content and delivery right.

His audience loved it, but only Chris knew how much he burned with excitement, how important it was to create a personal and compelling moment with his speech, and how eagerly he'd waited to perform.

To his surprise, he hadn't felt the least bit of stage fright. I've seen people freeze up when delivering to groups no larger than twenty. But his experience was different. He told me he'd felt a rush as he prepared, a feeling generated from picturing the people in the crowd looking up and being pulled away from whatever they were doing. He constantly imagined bringing them into the story.

"It was just a toast," Chris said. "So, in a lot of ways, I had nothing to lose. Most people would forget a poor toast and, with all the other things going on that day, it was not high priority. But it meant a lot to me. I really went for it that day. There I was on the stage, in front of 700 people, safely behind the microphone, telling the story the audience didn't realize they had come to hear. The one that would add another layer of meaning to an already meaningful experience."

After that speech, a friend had made a casual comment. "Dude, that was really great. You should be a motivational speaker." An off-hand comment that, in a brief moment, began to change his life. His mind opened to the possibility of doing just that in a larger capacity. What if it was more than a wedding? What if he could do this for an audience larger than the class he taught in the juvenile corrections facility?

"Maybe the lack of stage fright comes from having been frightened so much before," he told me.

He had been making his living as a teacher in a juvenile corrections facility for about three years at this point. I was interested in what he meant by afraid, so I asked him to go on.

"When I first started teaching, I was terrified. Some of these kids were only three or four years younger than I was, and pretty intimidating. I had no idea what I was doing. Sure, teaching, but we had to do much more than that, we had to get kids to change their behavior.

"Over the last three years I've been called every name in the book, I've had students ready to fight or throw something at me for telling them what to do. I screwed so much up in the beginning that I wasn't sure if I should continue teaching. But I kept on trying, coming up with different strategies, and with some great help I've learned to be very effective with them.

"I think I don't have stage fright because there is nothing these guys can throw at me that I haven't seen before. Adults are easy. The same philosophy that informed my work with juveniles can pull me through any situation with an adult."

He loved his experience with the kids, he loved teaching, and talked with me all the time about them, their achievements, and how he wished, at the same time, that he could find a way to have a bigger impact. The speech seemed to have helped open the door to an answer to this question.

"My time with these kids is starting to make me believe I can have a bigger impact. Like maybe I can take what I learned about how to approach them, how to allow them to be heard, and bring it into the business world. If I can get a 16-year-old kid who was defiant, violent, and drug addicted to change his behavior, I can do it with adults and larger groups as well."

When he talked about motivational speaking, he spoke faster and more earnestly. He grinned and carried on the way people do about their first child. It was as if that moment at the wedding had given birth to something that only seemed new, but had been present all along. He said that, in the process of him sharing stories, it was as if his listeners were being brought back into their own story.

He found more places to talk almost immediately. Small groups, Rotary clubs, and anywhere that was interested in having guest speakers. He shared experiences in juvenile corrections, information about behavior change, and even a few running or rugby stories.

"It's like I can see the energy in the room," Chris would say. "It's like there is a pattern I can follow. I can tell when they are engaged by a lean forward or the absolute silence in the room. Then I'll pause and let the emotion sink in. A well-timed laugh becomes permission, and means it's time to go deeper. They seem to be thinking, we're on your side. At this point, it's like I have them, and it's time to give them what they came for, that emotion they've been hiding in their gut and covering with their insecurities. I just love the possibilities. I want to make them feel again, to dream again, and maybe even start believing again."

He had an air of confidence back then. Teaching in a juvenile corrections center had both given him purpose and opened his eyes to the possibility of having a bigger effect on the world. Each day was full of challenges. This desire to have a positive impact on those kids had encouraged him to start running. He quit smoking and signed up for races because he felt it would make him a better role model. When he lost twenty pounds and ran his first marathon you could almost watch the belief in his potential to have a bigger impact grow in real time.

This idea of being a motivational speaker seemed to present itself at just the right time. He was finishing his MBA and, while he enjoyed teaching, he knew the problem he was trying to help solve was bigger than the classroom. This impact idea, the desire to make things better for those kids, seemed to come from deep inside him. He had never fully articulated to me what was behind it, only that he saw speaking as a way of getting to the root of the problem by influencing the community. It felt like fate had intervened and asked him to do something bigger. Like the momentum of a wave coming to shore, his idea felt as natural as the water washing up on the beach.

As his coach, I knew that a wave could also wash up on the rocks just as easily. I worried about him losing his momentum. I tried to tell him how I thought it was a great idea as much as possible and that I believed he had the ability to become a professional speaker and be great at it. I had seen him build his confidence over the years from being successful in so many of his endeavors, but I also knew this one was a very big potential dream for him. Maybe bigger, in his mind, than anything he had tried before.

He never told anyone how the compliment had made him feel. He didn't even share with his wife the image that had formed in his head that day. Despite all the confidence he seemed to bring to everything else, for the first time he began to doubt, to shy away from an idea even briefly. It was a small hesitation that would have a big impact.

Almost as quickly as the dream had come the process of it slipping away had begun without either of us noticing. A pattern I've learned to identify much more quickly since that time.

While Chris would never admit it, even to me, I knew he had worked hard to present a certain image. Like everyone, in some form or another, he needed recognition and depended on the outside world to validate his decisions to some degree. It helped him to know what path to follow and to know he could count on getting positive reinforcement throughout.

What seemed to him like sound choices, logical decisions balancing "reality" and "risk," were really the hedging of bets. Death by a thousand cuts might just begin with a scratch. As quickly as the idea had come, so did the doubts.

"Being a motivational speaker is a fun dream but not what you do when you have just finished your MBA," he rationalized. "I've already gotten a lot of flak for being a teacher, like I didn't have a real job. Being a quote, motivational speaker, would just make that worse. If, however, I can use the same skills in the business community, then it will have value. What if I looked for jobs that would allow me to speak and/or employ behavioral change techniques? Speaking to the small groups that I have invited me lately is fun, but I need something real."

I was caught off guard initially.

"Chris," I said. "You can do this! It's the most excited I've ever seen you. Why not just go for it?"

"Maybe because I don't want people to roll their eyes," he said. "I see two kinds of people in motivational speaking; either lovable losers like Chris Farley's van-down-by-the-river character on SNL, or the ridiculous success of someone like Tony Robbins. I really doubt that kind of success is going to come out of Boise, Idaho, from some young guy whose only experience is being a teacher and running a marathon.

"I want to help people, but I need it to be legitimate. I'm thinking about being a financial advisor. It seems like the best of both worlds. I can help people change their behavior, identify their values, and achieve dreams. It's the same thing, just with money, financial products, and things that have value. Helping people with their money, with legitimate financial products, is real, and there are plenty of examples of people doing it around me."

And as quickly as we had the conversation, he had a new job. Within weeks of having the idea he took the tests he needed, quit his job, and became a financial advisor. When he decides there is something he wants, it's crazy how fast he can go and get it.

I hoped that this was simply a step toward becoming a speaker. Initially, the conversation sounded more like he was exploring options, but before I knew it he had made the decision and was on his way. I wasn't comfortable with how fast everything was going, nor was I sure he had thought everything out. But I was curious about where he might take it.

***

"How's the new financial advisor job, Chris?"

"Honestly, I'm hooked. We're trained to ask a simple question: What's important about money to you? I like it. It's a way for people to feel like they have some control and ownership in the process, and move toward the values they find most important."

I watched him work hard, redefining the question and the process. I could see he went deeper than expected with clients. He was genuinely interested in what they wanted and what that meant to them. Was it just a house or was it really a vital symbol of security? How could money help his clients be better husbands, wives, and citizens? With his knack for connection and deep instinct for the human experience, Chris drilled through surface financial questions to the real issues.

I could tell he approached adults the same way he was taught to approach kids. He was determined to make a difference for them. He listened, truly listened, reflected their words and behavior, and asked them what they really wanted deep down. It was like he was trying to help them find something they didn't know was available.

I ask him about his approach.

"It was the first time I was challenged directly by a student. I cared very deeply about getting them to change. So, when one of my most talented kids told me that he was still going to use drugs when he got released, I took it personally. I spent all my time and effort trying to convince him of how bad they were, telling him where those decisions would lead, and doing everything in my power to show him what he needed to be successful. Only to find that none of those strategies worked."

"What did work?" I ask

"After struggling for so long trying to be the expert for these kids, I finally had someone pull me aside and introduce me to a different approach.

"Sal was the guy's name. He had been working with kids for well over thirty years and was excellent. His interactions with the kids seemed effortless, like he knew what they were thinking before they did, and trusted him enough to do whatever he said.

"I was telling Sal about the trouble I was having with this kid, how I had tried to show him everything but he just wouldn't listen. I laid out the whole case to Sal hoping he would find a piece of information I had forgotten to give to him. Only, after I had told him the whole story, he simply asked me a question."

"What question was that?" I know that this is the important piece.

"When is the last time you asked this child what he wants?"

"That seems like an odd question." Thinking to myself that the answer should be obvious.

"It seemed like a ridiculous question. I told him the kids obviously don't know what they want, or they want the wrong things. Why else would they be there?"

"Seems reasonable to me."

"It did to me as well. Until he explained it fully. He asked me how I could possibly believe a person could change, to do or be better, could improve their situation, if I didn't believe they had all the tools necessary within. All the potential inside themselves.

"Educo, he used to say. It's the Latin root of the word education. It means 'to draw without, or extract from.' If I was going to have any chance of reaching these kids I had to believe in their value, not just the value of the information I had to share. I had to trust them, know they have the potential, or none of the fancy information is going to be of any use." You could see him light up just talking about the approach.

"I assume it worked for you?" I ask, knowing the answer already.

"It turned my teaching around almost overnight. Not to mention helping me find strategies to work with that kid. I had to believe in him, trust his value, before the information would have any benefit. It's the same thing I now do with these adults."

It was a powerful concept, Educo. And it was exciting to listen to him talk about it and apply it in different contexts. Instead of pushing information into people, he believed it was about pulling the genius out of them. Educo told him they were potential waiting to be brought out to the world.

"How does that apply to finances, Chris?" I ask, wanting to bring him full circle.

"That's the beauty. I'm not telling people what they should do with their finances. I can see that my job is really to extract from them their dreams, to pull from them their values, and bring to the surface what they feel is their bigger purpose. If I can do that, then the finance piece becomes easy. We simply connect one to the other. Where other people focus on telling their clients what to do, I simply focus on what's important to them, what they do well, and connect the products in a way that helps them feel like they are in control. Because they are, or at least they should be, and following the Educo philosophy allows the decisions to take care of themselves. Educo lets them lead the show."

"Sounds incredible," I say. I believe I was more excited than he was. "I really think you could use this as a speaking concept and get paid to talk about it." I try again to get him to see what I thought he could do.

But the strategy doesn't work. He simply shrugs his shoulders and again starts talking about what he needed to do to be a successful advisor.

3
GIVE AWAY

With each passing week, we talked less and less about his motivational speaking dream. His focus on being successful as a financial advisor had quickly taken our full attention. There were moments I wanted to tell him that the financial advisor job was a distraction. But I kept the thought to myself. You can only push a client like Chris so far. He needed to figure it out for himself.

Turns out he was a good advisor. In true Chris fashion, it didn't take long for him to get itchy. He left that firm and started his own business, using his new approach of values-based financial planning as something of an indirect marketing tool to talk with people about financial service products.

His clients loved the process. When he created workshops, and delivered to small groups, they gave him great feedback. They would tell him how the process had helped them talk to their spouses or business associates about money in a way they hadn't before. They were more confident about reaching their financial goals than they ever had been.

Chris was not charging for the workshops, however, except for situations when he submitted the course for continuing education in professional associations. When people would approach him after the course to praise him, it's like he couldn't hear what they were saying. He would assume they were interested in a product and begin talking about insurance or investments. From this point, the participant would lose interest and Chris would leave believing they had lost interest in him.

"C'mon Chris, your talents and process as a speaker have real value," I say in frustration, wondering if I was more upset about him not seeing it, or that fact that I was not able to get him to see it. "You should be charging for the workshops as well."

"In this business, everyone tells me the products are how you make the money," he says. "If you get to speak, you should have a connection to the product. That's what the successful people in the industry do."

I had no idea who these other people were. I did know they seemed to have more of his attention than I did, and I was the one he was supposed to be coming to for advice.

Eventually, it always comes up with my clients. Everyone has a point where trying something new creates too much background noise, and they shy away. With Chris, that background noise made it hard for him to hear my, or anyone's, real encouragement.

"I'll grow the speaking side of the business after being successful on the product side," he says defensively. "After I've achieved the financial success that will make me legitimate."

It sounded reasonable, like a very thought out, risk averse plan. He has a way of convincing me of just about anything it seems. But while he viewed it as a simple strategic decision, I started to see it more and more as him avoiding a confrontation with his own doubt, discomfort, and nervousness. The guy who spent so much time trying to help other people see their own value didn't want to convince anyone else of his own.

Despite these discussions, there were days that he would show up to a session overwhelmed with excitement about the workshops he had developed. "I have to tell you about this last group I had…" I had gotten used to the bursts of enthusiasm and they were quite entertaining. I would never, however, get used to the discomfort of knowing he wasn't connecting that excitement to his real dream, especially given how close I felt he was to having it realized.

I settle in for his latest story.

"Ok, so I got a call to teach another group of real estate agents. And, while the workshop itself is no different than any other I've delivered lately, there was this one guy…" He pauses momentarily, then continues with the energy of child. "Wow! I think it was one of the most intense workshops I've ever delivered."

"What happened?"

"During my time in juvenile corrections, I developed the skills and tools necessary to deal with hostile reactions to the content I am delivering without getting thrown off course. I had to utilize all of them when an individual in my workshop started the day by directly challenging my abilities. A farmer in the front row asked me, 'What the hell are you going to teach me about managing my business? I've been doing this since before you were born.'

"Turns out he was a 55-year-old farmer and business owner with more than ten million dollars in real estate who ran a small farm and had his real estate license only because he wanted to know, and perhaps control, as many of his own transactions as he could. He fit the description of self-made man perfectly. In terms of business knowledge, we both knew the answer was likely, not much."

"Sounds intimidating," I say.

"More like irritating," Chris says. "Let's be honest. I haven't been getting the traction on the product side of the business that I had hoped initially. Now this dude is going to try to challenge what I know? I wasn't having it. So, instead of giving him the standard 'everyone gets something different' response, I told him that if he didn't get something out of the next three hours, I would give him his money back. I know I needed the money, but I didn't care. I knew I could provide on the workshop side, and raising the stakes just made me feel more in control."

"That's a pretty brave move," I say, anxious to hear how it went.

"When the workshop finally started, I worked the twenty participants as hard as I knew how. I trusted them to come up with their own strategies even if we had to sit through some uncomfortable silence. I knew they had the answers, and I believed they were going to find a way that worked for them. You can teach patience and reading the audience, but believing in them is something you must do with faith. You can't fake that."

"I'd never really thought about that. But it makes perfect sense,"

"I've found that facilitation is less about delivering content and more about understanding the group well enough to make the content work for them. I never believed I had any new information, because I don't. But, somehow, I've always known how important it was to make the information work for the people in front of me. If I can connect it to their value, to the things they believed in, then there is a good chance it'll stick. They call them 'Aha Moments'; it's what speakers and facilitators desire most for people to have in a workshop. People think it's about hearing a new and different idea. The Educo idea makes me believe it is more about when an idea you may have heard once or a thousand times actually becomes personal, when you can see it working for you, and when you can see a new path forward through this idea. Like the fog lifting to reveal the glimmer of an opportunity right in front of you. That glow isn't from the new idea but from the fire created when the idea connects to the uniqueness of the individual. The light at the end of the tunnel becomes brighter when the internal fire is lit up. It's a reflection, not a destination."

I nod my head, captivated by his ability to pull me into a story.

"In the three hours of working with that group, lights seemed to kick on every fifteen minutes. I trusted them, or I simply stopped worrying about pleasing them. If that farmer was going to challenge me, he was going to get the full-frontal assault, gloves off and heart exposed. We went back and forth with each other, taking the group with us. The farmer asked, 'Why are we talking about personal values in business?' To which I fired right back, 'Well, has the sense of pride in having an honest business ever not been personal to you?'

"At times, I couldn't even tell who was the instructor. The group would hang on the farmer's questions as if hoping for an answer that would give them permission to make their own businesses more personal for themselves. He would ask questions to give validation to things he believed but had never really said out loud.

"The same tenacity that allowed him to ask the initial question was present in how he approached the class and how he ran the business. The part of him that wanted to be successful because of the difference he wanted to make in the community, the legacy he wanted to leave for his family and other reasons that were bigger than him was trying to get out. I was working the entire time to show him the door. His questions helped him see he had the key the entire time. We opened the door together."

"So, did he ask for his money back?"

Chris shakes his head.

"No, he didn't. In fact, he gave me his card and told me to call him."

"That's awesome," I say, thinking this might be just the experience he needed, to see the value in the workshops he was delivering.

Almost instantly, however, the passion that Chris had brought to telling me the story seemed to drain from his face. He looked down at the floor transitioning from victory to defeat in a matter of moments.

"What's wrong?" I ask, surprised.

"Deep down, I think he's right. There is nothing I could teach him about his business. I told him that I thought there were a couple of products that might work perfectly for his situation and the conversation seemed to go sideways. Like he wasn't really interested in the first place."

Chris's comment catches me off-guard. I don't know what to say.

"I really think I was just lucky enough to get him to see some things about himself during the workshop. I wouldn't know what to do if I started working with him as a consultant. I know he likely doesn't need any of the products I have to offer. Underneath it all, I have nothing to teach. Nothing that he doesn't already know. No, I don't think I'll be calling him after the way the conversation ended."

***

As I listened to him, and intermittently tried to disagree with him, I became convinced that his unwillingness to charge for the workshops had less to do with a business strategy and much more to do with his lack of confidence. Nothing I told him seemed to help him see that his unique delivery had value, and he should be charging for it.

It's a common problem with so many of the people I coach; they have a poor sense of their own value and that becomes what they charge, nothing. They give their services away for free believing that what they have to teach is a cheap commodity and they rob their clients of the opportunity to express their own values.

He had shown the farmer something about himself in that three-hour workshop and the farmer was interested in exploring it. Who knows how many times people get this opportunity, to be open enough to look within themselves at the same time someone is holding a mirror without judgment?

I tried to tell Chris he was robbing the person of this opportunity. I remember him looking at the card, promising me he was going to call. I know for a fact he never called, and I'll bet he forgot we even had the conversation.

Almost all clients come to a point where they don't want to move forward. Like a wall we hit without even knowing or seeing it directly in front of us. I could tell him thousands of times that he had the skills, the ability, and that he would provide great value to this person. But, the self-doubt was louder, and the louder voice always directs the attention.

We discussed the workshop he had put on and it was like talking about two completely different events. He talked about taking a chance and getting lucky with the client, while I tried in earnest to show him that it had nothing to do with luck. It was the skills that he had garnered and his natural ability to truly listen to them that made the impact for the participants, and specifically for this participant.

I couldn't tell if his responses were more discouraging for him or me. He would say that what he was talking about was nothing new and that people could get the information anywhere. I would tell him that it was not the information that was important, it was his ability to inspire people to apply it. The same reason he wanted to be an advisor, to help people find the motivation needed to change their behavior, was now something that he did not think was valuable.

When people make up their mind about something, it's pretty hard to change them. I spent less time trying to convince him of his abilities and he continued to avoid promoting himself, his consulting or his speaking. And, while he kept getting invited to do both, he began looking for something more tangible. Something he could offer his clients that would be worth promoting, and, I feared, yet another product to distract him from himself.

I remember sitting with him in those moments. Feeling like I was watching a truck driving straight into the side of a building, with nothing I could do to stop it but throw my body in front of it. And, in my response to him, it's exactly what it felt like I was doing.

"Chris, it's you! You're the one with the ultimate value. It's your value, man, not some random product that you don't even believe in, that people really want you to sell them. I'll just keep on telling you until it sinks in."

But the truck didn't as much as slow down. He wasn't listening anymore. All I could do was wait for the crash.

4
HIDDEN VALUE

When a coach pushes directly back on a client, they run the risk of creating a me-versus -you relationship. The client shifts their energy from proving themselves right to proving the coach wrong. As Chris entered the office full of excitement, I worried this was exactly the environment I had created.

Chris's situation had begun to deteriorate over the past six months. Selling something you don't believe in can be expensive. Yet, instead of changing his approach, he seemed to double down. He was delivering almost exclusively to real estate agents and had begun adding a real estate specific product to his sales mix, believing that things would change once he found the right product.

"I got a call from a real estate client of mine. She's been to one of my workshops before and really enjoyed it. Now she wants me to deliver my values-based business planning workshop to a group of 300 real estate agents, at their annual convention."

"This sounds great. Chris," I say with more enthusiasm than I feel. "People seem to really be interested in having you talk to them about this values-based stuff."

I was still desperately trying to tell him that he could make money doing the thing he cared about doing in the first place. His idea of working in the real estate field wasn't such a bad idea. It put him in front of people who really needed his consulting skills, the Educo process. Yet it still was not what he believed was the reason they were coming to see him.

"It will be the first time speaking about my ideas in front of an audience this large. They are going to pay me a surprising amount of money to talk for 45 minutes. I would have done it for free, given the exposure. There are likely to be some people I can actually sell something to at the event."

Hearing this, I just about fall out of my chair. I want to interrupt, but, honestly, I'm just too tired of having that conversation. Why should I bother? I've spent months showing Chris how much consulting and speaking could make him. I've watched people come to Chris, repeatedly, because they like him. They like the way he makes them think about their money and, more importantly, about themselves. But, it doesn't seem to matter, because he just gives it away for free in hopes they will pay for something neither of them care about.

I have to ask. "Will you just consider charging people for the consulting you're already doing?" If he could just connect this, he might see the opportunities sitting right in his lap.

He digs in his heels. "Look, I get it. You think I should be selling the consulting. But, as I've told you before, I think people will be much more open to talking to me about the consulting if I can prove value with the product."

"No one is calling you for the product, Chris. And you haven't made any money with it to begin with. Those products are distracting you from what you really want to do and, I believe, where you could make the most money. How much longer can you go on financially giving so much of what you do for free? You could be charging for this. You should definitely be charging for this."

"Hey, you don't have to tell me about my debt; believe me, I'm well aware. They're paying me for this talk, okay? And, who knows, maybe someone will want to buy a really large real estate investment and I will stay afloat for a couple months. But the reality is that no one in the industry charges for their time. They make money on the product, and, if I'm going to be successful, I need to do the same."

"C'mon Chris. The only reason other some people don't make money on the consulting is because they don't approach it like you. To them it is a sales tool. You actually believe the process can help people. But, for some reason, you think there is no value in helping people unless it comes with something tangible. Something outside of you.

"You are leaving money on the table and right now, you have no money to leave. People are trying to pay you and you refuse to see it. You have everything you need to stay afloat right in front of you, without any of those products. I just wish you would open your eyes to that."

I hate watching people sell themselves short. But it's something I see people do all the time. Because they don't believe in the value of their own skills, they fail to charge, or they severely undercharge, for their time, their advice, or their expertise. They look outside of themselves and sell or do things they don't really believe in or that don't inspire them. The position or product would be great for the right person; they just don't realize they are not that person.

To charge for our talents means acknowledging that our talents have value, and that we have value. People spend years becoming exceptionally skilled at something secretly hoping that someone else with tell them what it's worth, perhaps create a job for them, discover them. Yet the only person that needs to truly discover them is the one looking at them through the mirror each day.

People hide their passions, talents, and real value believing that work should be hard, that what you love can't be what you do, or that they can't feel good without feeling guilty. Because we value it internally, because the action itself is validating to us, we begin to believe we should discount it, charge less for it, reduce its value. We ignore or turn away the opportunity to acknowledge the actual value. How can we receive compensation for something that already gives us such personal gratification?

I felt as though I had already utilized any argument that might convince him to see this perspective. This talk would give me one more chance to show him. To prove to him that those things on the inside were worth far more than any product. So, I paid close attention to the conversations we had leading up to the event.

"Well, I met the farmer again," he says with a smile at our next meeting.

He hadn't even let me know he was doing another workshop until just now, when it was over. I try to listen while attempting to figure out why he decided to wait and share with me after the fact. I work to hide the annoyance of him not seeking my advice.

"Before the big talk, I decided it made sense to put on a smaller workshop again in Idaho."

"That was a great idea." Maybe he is seeing things differently.

"These real estate courses are easy to set up. People always need CE credits and there are industry standards on what to charge."

That he is charging for it is music to my ears.

"It was the same room as before. There was that farmer, sitting in the exact same chair as he had one year earlier, only this time with a smile on his face. The same guy that had directly challenged my abilities before had signed up for the very same workshop. This time, he didn't even need the credits, but he had come prepared to get more than some simple completion certificate."

"What did he say?"

"Well, I start by asking if anyone has any questions or concerns, like I usually do. The farmer raised his hand and, to my surprise and delight, echoed the exact same question of the year before: 'What the hell are you going to teach me about running my own business that I don't already know? I've been in business since before you were born.'"

"Wow, what a moment!"

"I was amazed at how the farmer knew where we were going but was still engaged to find deeper meaning in his own answers. The rest of the group seemed to feed off this guy. He made everyone else dive deeper into their own reasons for running their business: to take care of those they loved and make positive change in the world."

He is intense and excited. This is the Chris who can move mountains and overthrow empires. I push for the whole story.

"Sounds like an awesome experience, Chris. Did anything happen after the workshop ended?"

"The guy approached me after we finished and gave me his card again."

"What did he say?"

"He asked why I hadn't called him back last year, which I thought was odd. I told him that it didn't sound like he had any financial needs, since he didn't need insurance and didn't have any interest in the stock market. Then he said something that threw me, he told me he had wanted to talk with me about helping him have the same conversation about his values with his family. I couldn't believe it. The guy knows more about business than I probably ever will, and yet he still wants to talk to me."

"Why do you think that is?"

It's time to change my approach. I have to be gentle here. I want to get him to see it himself. I'm still angry that he didn't listen to me months before, but if this experience will open his eyes, I'm not going to waste it. If he won't listen to me, maybe he'll finally listen to his clients.

"I guess it's my background. The process is so simple, though, I can't believe he couldn't look it up himself."

"He probably can, Chris. But he can't Google your belief in him. He can't find your commitment and passion to the process through some app, and whatever book he reads will not give him the inspiration your presence gives him. Your belief in him helps him find what he needs to believe in himself."

He considers my words. It's obviously a lot for him to take in. In this moment, I begin to realize it's more than a strategy I'm trying to convince him to buy into. It's a way of thinking, a philosophy, perhaps a belief that has to change. It's not how he views the product or service as much as how he views himself.

"Do me a favor, Chris. When you are speaking to this large group, I want you to look for it. Look for the connection you are making with the group and how they might be looking to you for permission."

"Permission for what?"

"To reward you for helping them connect with themselves."

The value of ourselves. It's not something we learned in school. I see my clients spend their entire lives relying on other people to set monetary value on their validation: here is what the job pays, here is what the school costs, here is what you can make.

Chris seemed to be stuck in that constricting view of value. Someone tells him how much he can charge, how much he will make, and even who he can and cannot sell it too. Totally quantifiable. Completely out of his control.

There was no chart on the wall to tell him how much he was worth. And, if there was, he wasn't looking for it. Chris didn't believe in the value of what he did outside of the feeling that it gave him, and perhaps gave others.

How do you charge for a feeling? Especially when that feeling seems to benefit you as much as the other person?

Actually, people do it all the time. Counselors charge for helping clients feel less anxious and improve their own self talk at the same time. Landscapers might quantify their cost based on goods, but what their clients really pay for is standing in their yard and feeling proud or calm. People don't simply buy cars, they buy the feeling they get when they sit in a vehicle that represents who they are or who they want to be.

And now, Chris was going to connect with those things that really drove him in a way he had never experienced before. In a way I was certain would finally open his eyes to his potential.

People work in the speaking industry for years trying to get the break he had just been given. It was his chance to speak on a larger stage and gain national recognition. It was an opportunity to showcase his coaching and facilitation skills in front of hundreds of potential clients. Opportunities surrounded him for the thing he really wanted deep down, whether he would see them or not was the question.

It just so happened that I could attend the event and

watch Chris on that big stage. And I was not disappointed.

"Watch for a moment when the room gets quiet," he had told me. "That means something interesting is about to happen."

I could almost feel that moment approaching. The audience was on board, but they needed a push. They would lean in, listen and write things down, but there was still a trepidation in their actions. They believed what he was saying but needed to connect to it.

C'mon Chris, I thought. This is it! Don't just show them, make them feel it.

He started with a question.

"Is there anyone in the audience brave enough to volunteer?" Chris asked. "The questions might be a little uncomfortable."

As always, he was setting them up for safety, letting them know what they were getting into so they could choose to be a part of the process.

A few people raised their hands. Bob, a prominent Realtor who'd invited Chris to talk, was one of them.

Chris walked to where Bob sat in the room. I swallowed hard. This moment was unrehearsed.

Chris encouraged Bob to stand up. He handed him a microphone and asked him the question he had used to start hundreds of powerful conversations.

"Bob, what's important about money to you?"

"Well, it allows me to pay for a house and provide for my family." Bob sounded puzzled, wondering where the discussion was headed.

"Now Bob, I know this might sound obvious, but what's important about doing those things?"

Yes, Chris, yes. Dig in deeper.

"I want to be able to take care of my wife and kids. That's my responsibility."

"What does that say about you, Bob? Why have you made taking care of your family such a high priority?"

Ah, Chris, that's it. Take his assumptions and bring them into the open. Don't take for granted this beautiful thing that Bob has chosen to do. Bring it out and recognize it.

"I suppose that's just about being a good father."

I could see in Bob's eyes that it was starting to get real. Like the rest of us, he'd probably been taking his decisions to act on his values for granted. But something happens when we look directly into those decisions. They become purposeful, meaningful, and quite beautiful.

"One more question Bob. You have been awesome so far and I thank you. But can you share with me why it's so important that you be a good father? Deep down, what does it really mean to you?"

Here was the moment he had been waiting for the entire time. He knew it, he was ready for it, the group was ready, they were simply a response away from realizing it too.

The room grew quiet. Chris had opened the door and waited for the invitation. Now it was time to make it real. Bob needed to connect to the part of him that was on fire. He needed to reach into the core of himself that is responsible for moving the rest of him forward. What meaning was he making in the world?

The audience waited. Everyone was on edge, wondering what would come out of Bob's mouth next and hoping he would have the courage to be vulnerable. We all longed for him to say what he really wanted out loud, to put it out in the world, to proclaim it, and to acknowledge he was worth it. He was speaking for all of us.

Bob took a deep breath and looked down. Slowly, he put the mic to his mouth and raised his eyes to ours. We watched him step into his own and unapologetically deliver what was in his heart.

"Six months ago—" He paused for another breath. "—my father passed away."

I swear, everyone in that room inhaled and then just held their breath. The moment was bigger than anyone had anticipated.

Bob continued: "I've thought a lot lately about what it means to be a father and who I want to be for my child and my wife. If I can be a fraction of the man my father was to me, well, I guess that's the most important thing in my life right now. I want to give my kids what I had. Not just financially, but emotionally, and spiritually. Being the best father I can be to those kids, giving them the chances I've had, it means everything to me."

His eyes filled with moisture and his chin came up at the same time. It was a proclamation. He was owning his space, and he had just reinforced his direction. A single tear of vulnerability fell down the most invincible face you've ever seen. It was unapologetically Bob, courageous enough to be completely exposed.

This was an important moment for both Chris and me. We connected that day in a way that strengthened our relationship. I got to truly witness his value first hand. I wanted him to understand the admiration, pride, and trust I had in him. I'm not sure I had done a very good job in communicating that before.

The conversation set the tone for the rest of the workshop. It was incredible. People began creating their own plans based on the most important values in their own lives. Bob had shown the way and, with his example, they were now one thousand percent engaged.

When people burn for something, and when they get really clear about what is most important to them, it's delicate and powerful at the same time. It's like being enveloped in a wave, surrounded by energy, floating weightlessly with complete power to choose any direction at the same time.

When it was over, Chris had helped develop meaningful insights for Bob and the group in one short hour. He started to see how valuable his skill was, perhaps for the first time.

"So, what do you think that was worth, Chris?"

"What do you mean? It was obviously worth just what they had paid me to do it."

"No, that's simply what the meeting planner had paid you to do it. What do you think it was worth to Bob, the rest of the people in the audience, or even Bob's family?"

"How do you quantify that?"

"So, you're saying you see it?"

"Sure, I do. But how do I put a price tag on it? I get as much out of it as they do. I would do it for free because it gives me that feeling as well."

"How much would you pay for that feeling? What is that worth? And, for you, wouldn't you find more value in it if you got to pay for it?"

Chris paused, as if considering it for the first time. He didn't have an answer. Neither of us needed one.

It's one thing to do something we love. But without allowing others to communicate how much they value it, whether through money or some other means, we can rob them of their experience. Chris didn't have to wait for someone else to define that worth. His eyes were opening to this for the first time.

Looking back, I often wonder how things might have been different if I had helped him see this earlier. What could

I have done to open his eyes to what was sitting right in front of him, to his own potential?

People approached him after the workshop to ask for help. Just like the farmer—all he had to do was call them back. With that, and a couple large speaking gigs under his belt, he was on the verge of having a speaking and consulting business most people wait years to create.

Unfortunately, he was also $70,000 in debt.

It had all happened so quickly.

That's the thing about jumping off points. They can disguise themselves as the end. Which sometimes they are, depending on how you choose to define them.

Chris was at his launching point and couldn't see it. Without wings, the cliff looked more like certain death.

Validation is important. Knowing the value we deliver can open our eyes. But it's only part of the puzzle. And pursuing the dream is not without consequence, as Chris was about to learn.

If only I could have helped him see earlier.

How different things might have been.

5
DREAMS

What had prevented Chris from opening his eyes sooner? This question haunted me. What had I missed? Why couldn't I get through to him earlier? I had to take a step back. It's as if it was clear to everyone but him. I played back all of our prior discussions in my head, reviewed my notes, and even listened to a number of the conversations we had recorded. Hearing your own words a second or third time can give big insights into the underlying thought process.

It didn't take long for me to realize what I was missing. Stepping back to look at the big picture and doing my best to listen to what he was saying behind the words that were actually coming out of his mouth, I began to understand.

He was scared.

He had been afraid since the beginning. Only now, maybe indirectly because of this focus, he had created tangible reasons for his discomfort. Namely, 70,000 of them: American dollars, all owed by Chris to a series of banks with a high interest rate. His fits and starts had caught up. And this debt was all the more frightening to him because it was a private misery; one his wife did not yet know about.

To make things even worse, this was 2008, right in the middle of the economic upheaval that changed so many people's fortunes.

Over the last four years, Chris had gone from doubting his abilities to a kind of internal paralysis in which he could no longer trust himself or imagine a better future. In short, he was petrified.

I'd been so focused on him getting the validation he so desperately needed that I'd forgotten the most basic of psychological needs—safety.

At this point, all the validation in the world wouldn't matter. Chris needed to get his head above water before he could swim.

It used to be a lot easier with clients. When I started coaching, most of the validation my clients searched for could be found in external process, or simply from other people.

In simpler times, you took a test, did well on the test, and moved on to the next level. Validation came externally, from passing the test and from the doors it opened. Clients would do this in a few different ways. They might get a certification in a specific field and find a stable job, become an apprentice and open themselves up to a great career, or get a Master's degree to qualify for a promotion. Validation that ultimately relied on others, but almost always led to a reward.

While these qualifications and certifications are certainly still available, the consistency of the reward on the other side is not. The quasi-guarantee that once came with them is all but gone.

What most people miss, however, is that at the same time the old paths are getting less consistent, new paths are opening up. From social media specialist to life coach, from full-time blogger to professional video gamer, Uber drivers to Airbnb owners, and any number of new business ideas, new opportunities for validation are everywhere. Opportunities that do not rely on the externally dependent model. But they become hard to see when our brains are too busy being scared, stressed, or outright overwhelmed with immediate needs.

The exciting part of the last few years was that Chris was on the brink of creating one of these new paths himself. He was attempting to change the way people approached financial and business consulting. What held us both back was the lack of guarantee, or the simple belief that we still needed one. When you are so focused on finding security, you almost always miss the opportunities to create it yourself. It's hard to find what you are not looking for in the first place.

There was no template for creating this new path that he was aware of. Sure, other people had done similar things that he could and should learn from, but there was no certification that would assure him what he was doing had value, and give him the confidence to charge for it in the future. He wasn't trying to build a foundation, he was attempting to find one already built by someone else.

To make matters worse, I was scared myself. My reputation was on the line. I encouraged him to focus on the financial services and real estate products because I'd seen people be successful with them before. It was plug and play, follow the path. I encouraged him to get every certification he could: financial, real estate, consulting, you name it.

In fact, now that I think about it, Chris might have been the most qualified and least-paid person in many of the rooms he entered. We spent so much time seeking his value through the paths laid out by other people that he couldn't see a potential new path, one we could create together.

As I look back, it is easy to identify my own blind spots. I believed in his potential, knew he had so much to bring to the table, but I could never convince him of it in a way that got him to see it himself. I thought I focused on those certifications and qualifications to show him how much potential I believed he had, he thought he needed them to hide something he lacked.

I once had a psychologist tell me, "you can't teach psychology." I was annoyed because that's exactly what we do as coaches. Whether we're trying to nudge a friend into making a better choice, a child into believing in themselves, or a client into changing their life, it all has some connection to what's happening in the person's brain.

But you can't teach it. Well, you can, it just probably won't help, which was really the guy's point. When it comes to changing behavior, knowing what to do has little value. Everyone knows how to quit smoking, they know how to work out, we know how to save money. Whatever behavior you are trying to change, the knowing how is the easy part. You can know psychology and never change your behavior.

It's in the doing, which starts with believing, that gives psychology its value. It's an applied science. People don't quit smoking because they suddenly realize it is unhealthy. They knew that all along. They quit because they work to apply this knowledge against their daily activities. Which is where knowing psychology, or how the brain operates, becomes quite handy. They begin to take advantage of opportunities to be this new person in their daily behavior. Understanding how the new picture of themselves, new beliefs they are creating about what is possible, forms in the brain make the process much easier. When this happens, people begin to realize the immense value of psychology.

I wish someone had shared this with me while I was working for Chris. Or rather, because I was already aware of the concept, I wish someone would have asked me if I was applying it with Chris. Because I wasn't. I was trying to teach him but not giving him the opportunity to apply. Telling someone they can ride a bike is much different than the feeling of freedom that comes with gliding down the road with the wind in your hair for the first time. I had been trying to tell him something he would need to experience to believe.

We all need validation, both generated from ourselves (internal) and received from the outside world (external), to have any chance at continuing a behavior. Our brains are designed to save energy. It does this by creating habits over time. If an activity has consistent validation, smoking and fitting in, running and crossing the finish line, saying hi and being acknowledged, then, over time, we begin to do that activity without thinking about it, using as little energy as possible. The more connected an action is with a validating response, the higher likelihood we will continue that behavior.

To keep our brain from using too much energy, we are constantly on the lookout for validation. If there is no reason to do an activity (validation) then we are just not going to expend any more energy toward that activity. The brain wants to save energy. If there is no reward, real or perceived, for the behavior, it will have a very low chance of being continued in the future.

Because Chris was only on the lookout for one specific type of validation, the kind provided by others, he failed to acknowledge the experiences that made him feel great that were happening along the way. It wasn't that other forms of validation weren't available, he simply wasn't putting any value on them.

His singular view of validation blinded him to the reality of the business he was creating. One that was unlike any he had heard about, worked for, or studied before.

I remember one visit with Chris at his house. He'd sounded despondent when he asked me to visit. Now that I'm here, he just looks beat.

"I've been spending hours sitting right here looking at two piles on my desk. All of my debts from the business in one big pile and business cards in a pile right next to them."

"Chris, you just spoke in front of a very large group of people and you have a bunch of others that want to do business with you."

"I know, and I want to believe it. I do believe it. I know I missed out on a lot of money. At the same time, I have to do something about the debt. I can't keep going on like this. All I see are the bills and it's keeping me up at night. I'm pretty sure my business is done. It has been for a while but I haven't told anyone about it. I just haven't accepted it until now."

"So, what are these piles on your desk?" To me, sitting here with fresh eyes and an optimistic outlook, I see opportunity.

"That is the 'could have been' pile. I have finally realized what they represent, but it's too late now, I can't take the continued risk of pursuing them."

"And what's that on your computer screen?"

"This? It's my resume. I just can't afford to have any more financial uncertainty. My next move is to hit send on this job application. It's not the right time to try to create a speaking and coaching practice given my current situation. The real estate talk was fun, but I just need to get a real job now. I have to get off the rollercoaster."

"Well, Chris, if you aren't going to follow up on those leads, maybe getting a job is the best thing for you right now. The question I have is, now that you realize that your skill set has value in the market, what kind of job are you going to find?"

As I wait for his reply, my eyes turn to the bookshelf. It holds an enormous collection of books, with titles like "Think and Grow Rich" and "Seven Habits of Highly Effective People." I can see at least 50 other books on goal setting and personal growth, along with strategy, finance, organizational development, education, psychology, and cognitive behavioral change.

He gestures wearily at the wall.

"Knowing all of this stuff was supposed to make me an expert. I've got more certifications, read more books, and have everything but a PhD. Yet I still feel like a colossal failure given the economic situation I've put myself in."

"You are not a failure, Chris. You just have to get your feet back under you. You've now learned that what you do has value in the market. You now know that everything you have worked on can eventually pay off."

"I did find one interesting job." He replies as if he had not heard what I had just said. "I have to check to see if it's real, and it does look like it would require Lynn and me to move, but I think it might be a great fit for me."

"Well, you seem to know what you need right now."

"Look, I get what you're saying about following through on the business leads here on my desk. I mean, I understand it logically, but I can't tell you just how exhausted I feel. Shutting the doors on the office was a big deal. Seeing these bills come in each day is like getting kicked in the stomach over and over. I just need something to feel better, to find my confidence again, so at least feel like I can breathe a little."

It wasn't just about validation anymore. He—we, really—had created a situation where validation was secondary to security. And just as he had sought validation in the paths of others, he attempted to find security externally as well.

Dreams are only as real as a client's ability to believe in them. With no belief, there is no vision. From the brain's perspective, survival is more important than hope, and so pain of failure recalibrates our goals.

Should I, could I, have pushed Chris a little more? He seemed to be aware of the value he could deliver. He had clients lined up in that pile on his desk. Maybe he was already over the hump? I wanted him to create more moments like he had with Bob. Interactions where he was completely engaged, at the top of his game, and making an impact. Delivering value on his own terms.

But the allure of this job he'd found was too great. He said it felt legitimate, validated by someone who owned a real business, and maybe it could be a safer path to eventually doing what he loved.

Dream Manager was the title of the position. I begged Chris to check it a couple of times to make sure it wasn't another, "all you need is $2,000 and you can become a…" kind of job. He called the company and did his research. They were going to hire someone to be an internal consultant for all of their employees. It involved holding classes and meeting with people once a month to help them get their own financial, career, fitness, or other goals on track with the idea that it would help them become more productive workers.

He told me it was like he was stranded on a deserted island and he was seeing a ship on the horizon. Perhaps he was supposed to find this job. All these papers sitting in front of him said he was perfect for the position, even the debts. If nothing else, he had certainly invested more than the other candidates.

Unlike with the cards on his desk, when he sent his resume and followed up on this job, he knew he was certain he would land the position. The validation he had given himself in speaking was carrying over to his job search, whether or not he realized it. To him, it was serendipity. It was meant to be and all was not lost. It wasn't a job, it was a lifeline. And that idea alone should have been warning sign for both of us.

It was an experimental position in a company that was less than five years old. He was in a relatively new industry, something about sales and coaching, and should expect some turmoil. Having worked with many clients in newly created positions, businesses, and industries since my dealings with Chris, I know now how volatile they can be. Couple that with

Chris's desperate need for security, something he hoped would be provided from this job, and it was a recipe for disaster.

Chris packed up his entire life and moved to Denver. We communicated sporadically. There seemed to be things we could talk about and things he avoided. We certainly could not talk about this person who had hired him and my concerns about how he was running the business. There was no mention of what Chris might want to do in the future, nor of the economic collapse. He was in survival mode and his focus was like tunnel vision.

Instead, he told me about what was happening day to day. They had anticipated 25 percent of the workforce would make an appointment with the Dream Manager; yet instead, in the first two months they had signed up more than 75 percent of the eligible employees. He enjoyed the flexibility to design the program for future use, bringing his background and skills into the picture.

We discussed how much fun it was to tell people what he did. When he told someone he worked as an employee coach within a company, they would say, "You mean HR." To which Chris would reply, "No, much cooler than that." He loved it. Someone had given him a shot and he was going to take it.

As excited as I was about the position, I worried about the recurring themes. When he was speaking before, he looked to outside processes and certifications for validation. Again, externally. The only difference with this job is that it was now security and validation.

He didn't need a job to do the type of coaching he was doing inside this company. He could easily have approached 100 different companies as an independent contractor and made this his own small business. But the job, a seemingly stable position provided by someone else, made him feel more secure. A feeling he did not seem to know how to provide for himself.

Our primal need for security makes us overlook the obvious flaws in our decisions. It's like losing a boyfriend or girlfriend. Our ego becomes so damaged that we start dating the first person who comes along. We overlook the obvious problems, convincing ourselves that the red flags are no big deal. We set ourselves up for an even bigger letdown. We just have to drive the stake a little deeper before we can acknowledge the pain.

I've seen my clients accept jobs way below their qualifications, convincing themselves that things will work out. I've watched them enter situations that, given a clearer head and a little more confidence, they would never have gotten near. When we've learned our entire lives to seek security externally, if we feel it is at risk, we can do pretty desperate things to find it. Unfortunately, people can take advantage of us in these situations.

He called me at eight in the morning angry and somewhat despondent on the other end of the phone. I could almost picture him with his head down, shoulders dropped, like the poster boy for agony. As if waking from a recurring nightmare.

"What happened?" I ask, tentatively.

"Well, I'm no longer a dream manager. That dream is gone."

I could tell as much by the tone of his voice and I want to know the rest of the story.

"It all started off so well. Lynn and I had made the decision to wait a couple of months for her to come up. We wanted to make sure things were going to work out before she quit her job and came to join me. We were doing our best to be cautious with how we approached this transition. But I was so happy to have finally caught a break that it was hard to not simply go all in from the beginning. It felt as though I could finally be the husband I had hoped to be."

"You are a good husband, Chris. Go ahead."

"Then she came to Colorado with the last of our stuff in the truck. It was time for me to pay her back. I kind of felt like I owed her for the debt I had accumulated while her job was paying the bills before. We were coming up on our anniversary and, for the first time in a while, we were celebrating."

"So far, so good," I say, focusing on what had gone well while knowing the story was about to take a bad turn.

"On our anniversary weekend, we decided to visit a school Lynn was interested in attending. I watched her eyes light up, looking around at all of the possibilities like a young kid eyeing her presents on Christmas Eve. It was like we were supposed to be there and this job was going to be my opportunity to give her the freedom to explore she had given me. And she deserved it. We had worked so hard and waited so long. The rest of the anniversary weekend consisted of pizza and beer shared while watching a marathon of movies on a couch fort we built in the middle of the living room. The poor man's anniversary. We felt like we were finally stable."

I smile as I think of them there, so happy after such heartbreak, almost forgetting where the story was heading.

"The next day I went to work early, excited about all the possibilities and the future we were creating. When I pulled onto the company premises I noticed another car in the parking lot. I had a bad feeling, like a police cruiser was there to tell you something had happened to your loved one. Only it was about to happen to me. It was the head of HR, and it was six in the morning. I knew something was wrong."

"Ah, Chris," is all I can say.

"From there it was all a blur. Swipe my fob. Unlock the door. Keep walking. I had to tell myself to continue moving forward. What the hell was she going to say? Was something wrong with the company? We were recession-proof, right? Conversations flew through my head. Warnings. Writings on the wall. Turn the corner. My office door is open. Why is she in my office? 'I'm sorry…' It's the only thing I really remember about the conversation. They laid off thirty percent of the workforce and I just happened to be there first. Lucky me."

I am there, feeling every anguish with him. A feeling that is even more bitter when contrasted with the excitement of a fresh start.

"Anger. Sadness. Fear. In that order. That's all I have felt since that morning. The first two come and go, but the last one is omnipresent. It's like I have no control, like every decision is the wrong decision."

"What happened next?"

"I remember the drive home. I remember having to remind myself to breathe, the taste of bile in the back of my throat as I struggled to hold down breakfast, images of how Lynn would react dancing in my head. I called friends for advice, but I don't remember the conversations. I told myself everything was going to be all right, but I didn't believe it."

"So, what are you going to do?"

"I'm taking the regional manager position I'd turned down before I moved to Denver. It was pretty pathetic when I called them this morning, like I was begging them for a job. But I got it. It was the right thing to do. Even though the idea of coming back to face my friends, family, and community feels like forced humiliation. I want to stay there, Lynn wants to stay, but this is just what we have to do."

"Why?" I ask half-heartedly, knowing his answer.

"This is what I'm supposed to do as a husband. These are the things I am supposed to take care of, and I'm not filling my role. I don't have a choice, I need a job and I need one now. I can do well in the position, I know how to be successful in the role, I will just get over the fact that I am not going to like it."

He sounds less than convincing.

"This is the economy. I have to face the realities of the job market. Sometimes we have to settle, I guess. Quit being such a damn dreamer and get a real job, come back down to earth and just suck it up. Lynn is upset but she understands. The whole thing feels like a car wreck. The collision happens, the police arrive, reports are made, the tow truck drags off the car to the rental center, and you're in a new car before you ever realize what happened."

What seemed like his entire professional direction completely changed in less than twenty-four hours. Goals, plans, hopes and dreams completely redrawn in an instant.

In the aftermath of 2008, I had so many clients in this boat that the conversations began to blend together. The security they had gotten through doing what they were told and being successful on someone else's terms was gone. It left them wondering what they had done wrong.

Chris was one of the lucky ones, whether he felt that way or not. He had a job to fall back on when so many others didn't. In fact, he had a lot of options. He had a severance, was qualified for lots of positions and could even do some contract work between jobs if he would have just slowed down to think about what he wanted. These were elements that provided security that he had created, only, like validation before, he refused to see them as relevant possibilities.

He was in survival mode. If losing his business had knocked him down, then getting laid off was the finishing blow to any sense of value he might have created for himself before. In a time when he needed to plan, he was only reacting. When he needed the part of his brain designed to think clearly about a situation, he was utilizing the side designed to run away from a predator. Yet there was no real direct threat and no imminent danger, only the story he had created in the back of his head. He was living in fight or flight mode instead of plan and imagine.

That ability to imagine is about considering the future. It is an ability that only humans have: to able to picture something that is not currently available, make up a potential story, and work to make it real. Chris had a severance, some savings, and some time, but he acted as though he would be homeless tomorrow. In grasping for the closest solution, he was neglecting any possible new direction that would include any remaining part of his initial dream—where there was an opening before, there was now only a dead end. There would be no coaching or speaking, it was time to get a real job.

He had started to believe in his own potential, in the value of what he could deliver, if only for the briefest of moments. A week before he was talking about what he wanted to do, what he was excited to create, and allowing himself to dream.

Now, the only thing he could talk about was what he was supposed to do, what he needed to do. He said he had no choice and this was just the reality. He left no time for exploration, imagination, or dreaming.

Fear has a way of reshaping communication. Words can have multiple meanings depending on the context. But, filtered through the constricting funnel where fear sends all thoughts, the definitions we choose become quite limited. It's as natural to the brain as running away from a hungry wolf. A primal response designed to save us from being eaten. Only we use the same response when our ego is being attacked, when responding to unexpected change, or when our perceived ability to put food on the table is challenged. The part of the brain responsible for fight or flight steals energy away from the part of the brain needed for imagination and creation. It's an important and natural prioritization system designed to first keep us from being eaten, and then dream up a better future once the threat is gone.

Only in this case, as with so many of the clients I see in this situation, the only real threat was the one the client decides to believe. The speaking and coaching gifts he believed in just months before, were now identified in his mind as threats. They had led him down the wrong road, put his livelihood at risk, and now they needed to be forgotten.

We call it the wolf at the door for a reason. It's a danger we react to by shutting down any unnecessary systems and diverting all energy to avoid the pain and eliminate the threat.

Chris' response was primal, connected to every story he'd ever heard about who he was supposed to be and what he was supposed to do. The provider, the husband, the breadwinner—those definitions defined him. He had been told that work wasn't supposed to be fun, that it was hard, and that, eventually, we all give up our childlike naiveté and start doing real work.

Every time he chose to accept someone else's paradigm, his story lost power and the imposed reality gained strength. With every decision to settle, to accept, and to take the more traditional route, the value he had once felt he could deliver, looked more and more like fool's gold. There were really two wolves at the door, but only one was being fed.

People can react unpredictably when they're afraid. They generally don't act or think like themselves. Conspiracy theories start here and mistrust finds roots. Doubt and suspicion take the place of love. Reacting feels good. It numbs the pain, stifles the struggle, and removes the work involved in creating something new. In this survival state, trying to talk with a client is almost useless.

Validation and security are intertwined. They are vitally important, fundamental human needs that we constantly try to find. Yet, in that search, we unknowingly rely on others to provide them. The truth is, the only true security is that which we provide ourselves, the only validation that matters is the one that comes from inside. They are needs we can only provide for ourselves, job or no job.

When fear runs the show, we tend to take the easy route. As Chris and I were soon to understand, the biggest danger in taking that path is not failure, but success.

6
SECURITY

Months later, Chris is back for another chat. He's wearing running shorts and running shoes, and looks like he might have worked up a sweat recently.

"I started running again."

"How does it feel?"

"It's different this time. Before, you know I'd run half marathons, full marathons and an Ironman triathlon. I spent hours training and dialing in my heart rate, splits, and diet. This time, none of that really seems to matter. It's like I'm just running to chill out. I'm sure I'll do some races later, but right now it's the only place things quiet down."

His mood seems better, and I'm happy to see that.

"Last week, I went out at four in the afternoon."

"Mid-July? It's been hot out there."

"It was close to 100 degrees and the sun was beating down like a weight on my back. I found a completely exposed hill, free of trees or any other cover that might allow a reprieve from the burning sensation. I ground out six miles with a 1,500 feet elevation gain."

"That sounds pretty extreme."

"It's like my sanctuary. Baptism by fire. I ran as hard as I could to the top. My chest was pounding, and I was fighting off vomiting. My legs were screaming, shaking, moving forward as if they had no choice. Push. Run harder. Fall. Get up. Until the pain becomes numb. Until the screaming on the inside is let outside. Until I've paid the price."

"Paid the price for what, Chris?"

"For being such an asshole. When I run, I clear my head, calm down, and think a little better if only for a couple moments. I don't know why I am being such a jerk, but I am, to everyone. I know I am supposed to be happy, and I'm trying. I'm one of the lucky ones, I landed on my feet. I have a good job, a company car, phone, and security."

"You'll get there Chris. Be easy on yourself."

"It's tough though. During the day, I walk into groups and feel like people are talking about me. 'Is that the guy who lost his business?' or more directly with 'I thought you guys moved to be a dream whatever?' I can't tell if they are being curious or vindictive. They are being vindictive, I know it. So, whenever I can, I run. It's the only time I feel like I am in control."

"Slow down man, that's just your insecurities talking. Your brain is trying to protect you from the outside. You've been through a ton in the last three years. But I can assure you most of those thoughts are simply false."

"People keep telling me I'm not being myself. What the hell does that mean? I'm starting to think that they just don't know me. Not myself. Sure, if not being dumb enough to buy my own bullshit is their definition of me not being myself, then they are right. I'm not that person anymore, I'm not naive, I'm just a regular dude. They ask me what I do for work now and I don't want to tell them. It just doesn't feel like me, this job. And yet, I am starting to wonder who the hell I am. How many times do you try to be someone before you figure out that's not who you are? How many times will I be told no before I just accept that this may be as far as I go? I just need to learn to be happy where I am. It's a good job. I could be here for a while, maybe retire here."

"It's pretty common to get tied to an identity, Chris. But what you do is not necessarily who you are. You're a good person, motivated and passionate, and that's why you take things so hard. People care about you and that's why they are asking about your plans, about what you do. You took a shot. Most people don't even get that. You knew there were risks. The reality is that you are better off than so many people who go through something similar."

He stares off for a while before replying.

"I know it will get better. It already has. Maybe we get one shot at our dreams and I took that shot. I should be happy. I should be grateful I have the job I have. On the whole, I'm pretty lucky. We don't get everything we want in life and at least I have the safety of this position. I can provide security with the right job, and this job certainly fits that description. It feels like safety might be more important than any of my crazy dreams. I'll learn to be happy. At least I can go for a run."

He knew it was the right answer. The one people wanted to hear. Perhaps the one I wanted to hear as well.

So many times, when Chris came to see me, it was really just about calming him down. I had to get him to a point where he could see clearly, to plan, to look past the momentary threats that seemed to be all around him. All of these changes, perceived failures and challenges, would fire up the fight-or-flight responses in his brain, making it difficult to quiet the anxiety and look at the bigger picture.

At least he was running, and we could focus on that. His entire sequence about getting up the hill was as good of a coping mechanism as I could have ever recommended. I felt like the balance of running and this job would, in the long run, get him back to thinking clearly.

He knew how to assign value to sales and management. He didn't have to convince himself this was a process that was worth something. He negotiated well for his current salary and even had the potential for a generous bonus system. No more working for free.

Still, he was back to an approach to work that just felt outdated. Get the security from the job and the validation in outside activities. Go to the factory during the day and join the bowling team at night. This is the social contract of the industrial era. You don't have to like your job. You should probably be decent at it, but you certainly don't have to like it. If you can do your time, you get to have the security of knowing you are going to be taken care of, and that becomes all the validation you need to keep moving forward.

The industrial economy created a simple trade-off for most people. We traded our time and toil for security. As long as we followed the rules and found a good and reputable company, we gained predictability in return. This came in the form of income, consistency, and a general expectation that, if you did your job well, you would have a job tomorrow. When you followed the path, you got all the validation and security you needed, externally, dependent on the consistency of a boss, a company, and the entire industrial economy.

Chris now worked for a company that had been privately owned for 40 years. Everything appeared as if it would be around for the next generation or two, with the owner's sons lined up to take the business into the future.

And with Chris in this role, I was on familiar ground myself. I knew how to help him with his running performance. We could plan for big goals. I could help him dial in his training and focus him on the next race. He was in a position that included sales and management. I knew I could help him with his process and he would find success. It would take him a while to get over his losses and pay off his loans, but eventually, he could build himself back up in these jobs. It was a strategy we could both count on.

All the energy and passion he had thrown into becoming a coach and speaker he now threw into running. True to form, he was going to do something big with it. He couldn't just run; he had to run ultramarathons. Before, when he picked up running while he was teaching, he'd chosen to run marathons and eventually train for an Ironman. Having a big event to train for always seemed important to him. The big events made him feel like he was setting a good example, like he was part of something bigger, and that his actions had some sort of purpose. He shared his exploits with his students, his friends, and as many other people as he could. In his own way, this was his attempt to inspire them the way he had wanted to as a speaker.

Not everyone gets to do what they love. That's the simple and straightforward fact of the matter. He could, however, let his job fund something he loved to do, and running was just that something. He had a consistent position at a company that would provide him the security he had lost along the way. Soon, things would be easier, and he would be himself again.

The positive change in his tone was obvious a few months into his new gig.

"Coach, I'm actually pretty good at this job. As soon as things settled down from the move back, I really put my head down to get to work. Work, run, eat, sleep. It's important that I'm successful in this position and show other people that I'm not just some failure. Despite the setbacks in the last couple of years, this work is making me feel much better."

"That's really great to hear, Chris. They hired to you apply the things you had been teaching in your workshops and it sounds like that's exactly what you're doing."

"Absolutely. Sell the potential, communicate the value, and act with purpose as a leader. Values-based business planning works when you realize, as Simon Sinek says, 'People don't buy what you do, they buy why you do it.' I believe in the why of this business, even if I don't actually like what I am doing."

"You must be enjoying parts of it, at least."

"I suppose I like winning. I like the sale itself. The first account I won in the new position was intense. This business has long sales cycles with high potential that the accounts will not come through. It was the largest dollar amount I'd ever been responsible for selling at one time, and I was nervous. I spent the weeks leading up to the final presentation burying myself in the numbers, in organizing the presentation, in making sure every question that could possibly come up would be answered. There was a lot of fear associated with those big contracts, but I had running, and it seemed to help me focus."

"It sounds like you're doing a pretty good job managing the emotions that have come with this transition. I'm proud of you, man. I hope you see that it's paying off."

"Sometimes it's like I'm simply driven by an anger to produce. I'm still mad at myself for having gotten in this position. When I left teaching, I remember someone saying 'those who can't, teach' and it was something that's stuck with me ever since. It's the music that plays in the back of my head sometimes, making me believe were right, that I can't do this."

"How do you handle that when it comes up?"

"The louder the voices get, the more full throttle into the account and into my running I go. I prepare for anything and any turn that might be thrown at me from the client. It's like I'm not selling them anything, I am going in to convince them that this path forward is their only choice and any other decision is simply the wrong decision. I am selling for this new company with every bit of energy and conviction I can muster. And it's working. The first account felt like magic. Vindication, validation, proof. This was my counter punch, my get-back-off-the-mat. I had been down but not out and just struck a blow for the good guys."

"Tell me about how that went."

It's important he says it out loud. The more I can get him to recognize and connect to the feeling, the more it seems to grow, and his confidence seems to come back out again. I want all the details and he's willing to share.

"My boss and I got the answer before the meeting ended. The presentation went perfectly. I knew every question before it was asked, knew every objection before it was uttered, knew what they cared about most and made them feel like they could have it. 'When can we start?' was the only question. Bam, closed deal. We shook hands and walked out of the building. Driving my boss back to his hotel, I did everything in my power to maintain composure, to act like this was an everyday thing. 'Looks like we have some work to do. Good job. See you tomorrow,' was his only recognition of the sale and of my part."

"That's it?"

"I drove the car two blocks away, parked, and cried. This had nothing to do with the sale. I just hadn't had a win in so long I was starting to think I couldn't. I felt like I was back on track. The following week I ran my first race in a long time and I felt it again. Like I wasn't embarrassed to be in front of people for the first time in a long time. As long as I was selling, as long as I was running, I was proving I could do it. I was winning at the game set in front of me. People could see this. It mattered. I needed this."

Validation. It's like water in a desert. This feeling that we are wanted or needed is so primal that, if someone doesn't feel it for a while, having it back again can be quite emotional, like a long-lost love returning.

"So, you feel like you're taking a bit more control of things?"

"It feels like we're getting more stability. I've got a car, a house, and medals for the races I'm running. The money is consistent and our worries are starting to go away. Work, run, eat, sleep. Sure, I may not be home as much as Lynn would like, but at least we aren't struggling to pay the bills. I might even be a bit distant with friends and family, but at least I'm being someone they can be proud of. Maybe people were right, telling me how easy it would be if I just got a regular job."

It was great that he was winning. At the same time, I was beginning to realize something in that last conversation. In Chris's success, I was finding reassurance. When he struggled, it was hard on me, too.

I was pleased to see him doing so well in the new job and in running. He felt accepted instead of like an outsider. He talked about how nice it finally felt to fit in, to be normal.

At the same time, there was a rather curious behavior that I began to notice. When he talked about making a sale, he said that it felt as if he was looking around a room full of people and saying, "See? I told you I could do this!" But I could never get him to pin down who he was talking to.

Like a slow recovery from a horrible injury, he eventually began moving forward. He was starting to talk more, to interact in groups and speak up in meetings. He was getting his mojo back. He could finally settle in and focus on simply doing his job. There were no distractions about whether or not it was a real job, and nobody warning him of the dangers. He was legitimate here, normal, finally settling down like everyone else.

His desire for continued signs of success drove him to bury himself in his work. And when he wasn't working, he was running. The busyness felt good to him. It was his comfort, his security blanket, protecting him from those feelings that used to haunt him. He could dive into work and forget about everything else.

I knew Chris was working too much. I knew something didn't feel quite right. But I just didn't want him to stop. How do you tell a racehorse to slow down in the middle of the race? It just felt so good to see him getting back up again, winning again. My job was to help him succeed, and that is exactly what he was doing.

I wanted the success to be enough.

7
SUCCESS

When my clients are successful, I feel successful.

I know I'm supposed to separate those things objectively. That's what consultants are trained to do. But it just feels so good when they are doing well, like I may have had a part in the process. It gives my work meaning. Particularly in the intriguing case of Chris, where that connection was the strongest I'd ever felt.

Two years passed before we knew it. He had won a number of contracts and was doing great in the job. Having turned around a once-struggling region, he seemed to be getting noticed within the company. His running had progressed as well. In a typical week, he spent 50 hours working and 20 hours running. On both fronts, he prided himself on working hard and putting in the time, and it seemed to be paying off.

He sold bigger and bigger accounts and ran longer and longer races. He was preparing to bid on the largest contract of his life and run the longest race he had ever run. These were huge milestones.

The race was a 100-mile ultramarathon, a distance very few people are able to complete. It was the culmination of years of preparation, effort, and training.

The account was massive; the commission alone would be more than he'd made in all of the last five months combined. Just getting the opportunity to win this piece of business was testament to his immense dedication and effort. Chris had made every preparation for this big account. He had traveled to the client's location days early to acquaint himself with the site and make sure everything was in order. He had scrutinized every detail in the proposal obsessively, with numbers crunched and re-crunched and the presentation totally dialed. I was sure he would knock it out of the park.

He did talk a bit about not being home enough and other issues on the personal side, but that goes with the territory. If you want to be successful, you are going to have to sacrifice some things. That's just the way it goes.

As a consultant, I couldn't have been more proud. He was very coachable and very driven. He was a machine, fun to watch, like he was invincible and could keep going no matter what.

He's coming in right now. I know he's going to tell me how he won the account and finished the race. He's worked so hard for these things, and I'm excited to see the payoff.

"Chris!" I shake his hand enthusiastically. "How ARE you?"

"I don't know," he says, puzzled. "Crossing off these goals was supposed to be a turning point for me. I've pictured them happening a hundred times in my head."

It sounds like he's been successful, but something is off, way off. He should be celebrating, and instead he seems confused.

"I thought with big wins I would finally turn the corner on the difficulties of before. I'm finally following the rules."

"Following them? You're crushing them! C'mon, I'm on

the edge of my seat here, Chris. The race? The big account? How did things go?"

"The account was the first thing to happen. It ended up being much easier than I had anticipated. In fact, it seemed as though they had chosen my company for the contract well before I had even delivered the presentation. There had been some pretty big changes on the price side with my company. I was not sure what was behind it, but it made it pretty easy for the client to say yes. In some ways it was a bit of a letdown. I still felt somewhat victorious, I was definitely happy, but not the panacea I was hoping to find. Maybe there was just more I needed to do that I didn't know about yet."

"Sounds like you're going to get a pretty big paycheck Chris. I don't imagine that is a letdown. It seems to me that the sale feeling easy is simply a sign of how good you have become. Your work and dedication have simply made it easy. That's something to celebrate."

"I want to believe that, but I had a similar feeling after finishing my last race. Don't get me wrong, it was an amazing experience. It took over 29 hours of straight running. It took every ounce of energy I had to complete it. I wanted to quit more times than I could count. But I did it, I pushed through, I made it to the end. I crossed that finish line and I was overwhelmed with emotion. I knew I would be one in only 4,000 people in the entire country to finish a 100-mile race that year. It felt good to have achieved something so big."

"Sounds incredible."

"But there was a moment right after the race that really bothered me. I can't explain it, really. I had dreamed about getting a belt buckle, the award everyone covets for finishing a 100 mile ultramarathon, for years. It was a symbol of success, of commitment, of being part of an exclusive group. As much as I had wanted it, when the race director handed it to me at the end of the race, I didn't feel anything. In fact, I felt kind of let down. Like it didn't matter."

"Maybe it's just too close to the time that you finished. It means a lot that you have come so far. You're probably just overwhelmed with everything you've done."

He looks at me as if perplexed. Trying to believe what I was saying but not actually connecting with an idea that felt so foreign.

"I'm trying really hard to like this job. I should be happier about it, but something just always seems off. I can't get fully engaged. I keep thinking that if I reach the next level, maybe it will change my mind about what I am doing. On paper it's a fantastic gig, the kind where people make careers."

"Maybe you just need more time?" I try to provide some perspective.

"I'm sure you're right. It's just residual feelings from those more turbulent times. The check from this new account will change all that, I'm sure. The money that will come and the feeling I will get when the client signs on that dotted line will allow me to finally settle down. I'm sure of it."

"Is that all that's on your mind?"

"Yeah, one other thing. My time at home has been relegated to weekends for the last couple of months. I spent those weekends putting in the five or more hour-long runs that I need to train for the race. Lynn has been trying to tell me to slow down a bit more, that she wanted to see me and spend more time with me. But I just don't feel comfortable when I'm not busy. I promised her, once this account and race were over, I would make more time."

"I'm proud of you Chris. I hope you know that a lot of people are proud of you. You've come a long way."

To be honest, I was trying my best to keep a positive view of the whole situation. But this sense of discomfort seemed to be contagious. Chris wasn't the only client I had that was feeling this way. Since 2008, I'd been hearing it all the time.

"I look good on paper, but I feel dead inside."

"My resume is rock solid but, when I read it, I think it is talking about someone else. I wish it were talking about someone else."

"There are people who are lining up for my job, but I hate it, and if I knew of anything else to do, I would."

With Chris, seeing him head down the same road was especially frustrating. He was supposed to be the one I could count on.

People come to me to be successful. Success follows some pretty specific strategies, templates, and requirements. And my clients were successful. They were achieving the goals they had approached me to achieve: making money, getting the job, finishing races and growing businesses. These clients had hundreds of medals and awards, countless degrees and achievement certificates, had spent thousands of dollars in hobbies and activities and were achieving the kind of success other people envied. Still, they came back with the same theme. They were unfulfilled and unhappy, like something huge was missing.

I couldn't figure out what was still bothering them. They were doing well at their jobs, but when I asked them about engagement and satisfaction they looked at me like I had just shown them an alien. They were doing well financially, they'd found success and people looked up to them. Yet, underneath all of it, they couldn't care less.

Busyness keeps all the focus on what's next. Don't stop and look where you are, don't pause lest the bear catches up to you, and keep saying yes to others because you don't know how to say it to yourself. Chris and the others were living in a perpetual race, always focused on the next finish line, believing whatever they were looking for would surely be found around the corner up ahead. He had gotten good at what he was doing, but he hated it at the same time. The victories helped, but they were short lived. Each time he achieved more, he cared a little less.

Eventually, I would begin to understand how much this type of activity becomes just a poor mask for the things that lie under the surface. They cover up the fear and disallow the ability to dream. If Chris had enough things to do, then he wouldn't have enough time to think about what he could be doing. If he kept himself busy enough with little things, he couldn't be disappointed by his real dreams, the big ones creating that discomfort just underneath the surface. Busy is the drug that feeds the never-ending hope of expectations. If he could only get this done, then he could feel better. If he could only achieve this goal, then he would be on easy street.

"I thought once I reached this point, I would feel successful."

"What point are you talking about?"

"I've gotten to do some things that I thought were a pretty big deal in the last couple of years. I'm making more money than I ever have, landed bigger deals than I'd imagined, just finished the biggest running race of my life. It's nice to have money in the bank. I guess somewhere along the way, I just thought I would feel successful. But I don't. Worse than that, I really don't feel any better now than I did two years ago."

"You are on top of the world, my friend. You've been nailing every goal."

"I know, I know. But this security stuff you were talking about... I was thinking about it last week, and I really don't feel any more secure today. I know having more money in my savings account should help with this, and in some ways it does, but I can't say that I really feel secure. It's like, every time I get a big account, I have to instantly focus on the next one or the worry, the nervousness, catches up with me."

I appreciate the honesty, but frankly, what the hell do I do with it, Chris? My job was to help him succeed, and we did.

Now he wants some bow wrapped around it? If he doesn't feel successful from actually being successful, what's left? I begin to feel my own frustration bubbling to the surface. I've done what he asked me to, but he's still not happy. I try to keep my cool.

"I'm not sure what you're saying here, Chris. If you can't feel successful after being successful, when do you think you are going to feel it?"

"That's just the thing. Success has always been right around the next corner, right until I make it around that corner, then it's gone again before I ever get to enjoy it. I've run farther than I ever thought possible and the feeling didn't change. I've hit every goal professionally in the last two years and nothing changed."

His next line absolutely floors me. When a client hits your biggest insecurity, it's often hard to maintain your composure.

"I created everything I planned to create. But I'm not sure that I have created anything that matters."

"Wow. That's a big one, Chris. I'm not sure how I feel about it."

Inside, I felt exactly the same way. I was mad. All that work we had done together... now he was going to say it was worthless? Was he saying he thought our work together was worthless? For the first time, I began to question my own abilities as a consultant. It felt as though he would be setting a perpetually-rising bar that I could never help him over.

"Underneath all this is a deeper feeling I can't shake. I just know something is going to happen. The market will crash again, something will happen with this company or something will happen with me. I know I should have more faith in this company, but I don't. They're changing. I don't know what's going on, but I'm sure it won't be good."

"Look here, Chris. You might be overthinking things a

tad. Why not give this a break? You've been burning the candle at both ends. It'll get better. We'll come up with something. Why don't you just go get some rest for a while."

Another placating response. I didn't need more time; I needed a different strategy. Sure, he'd been working more than he should have been. Too much coffee, too little sleep, too little time with his family. And, yet, I knew that wasn't the real issue. He liked to work and he wasn't lazy. But he was disengaging more and more with each achievement, and neither of us could figure out why.

I hadn't paid much attention to Chris' comment about his company's future. He'd grown up without a lot of money, and I'd learned it was quite common for people with this background to always feel the bottom might drop out of their finances, that they would lose their jobs, or some other dire predicament would happen at any minute.

These irrational fears often get better over time. Continued success and planned time off can help clients become more rational. But the future would not wait. Within a week Chris was sent an ominous email. The company was going to be sold to one of their competitors, potentially leaving him without a job. At the bottom of the email he wrote, "I'm going for a run, I'll stop by and see you tomorrow."

8
NO GUARANTEES

Chris's breakdown hit me hard. The entire time he was telling me about his torn Achilles and the news of not getting his bonus, I just felt numb. When he finished talking about driving home and vomiting, and after I got him to commit to coming back for one more session, I went for a walk. I needed to think about what I could have done better, what I might have been missing, and why it was these experiences were happening with so many of my clients.

It was one of those times, in the business of working with people, that you begin to wonder if you're doing more damage than good. I knew that coaches, teachers, counselors, speakers, and other professionals that work with people often encounter this sometime in their careers. But I didn't think it would happen right after I'd helped a client reach such great success.

For so many of my other clients, it was simply about finding a new job or a new challenge. I tended to work with the type of people who wanted a lot out of life, and getting them fired up about the next big goal generally did the trick.

But Chris was different. He felt as if he'd already been out on his own and attempted something big. The idea of stepping back into the independent world was still too dangerous in his mind. For him, so many of my go-to strategies weren't going to work.

I needed to take a bigger look at each of his challenges with some perspective. Not just the challenges that Chris had been presenting, but those that had crossed so many of my other clients. What were the themes? What had changed? What was I missing?

I record a lot of my consulting sessions and thought it might be helpful to go back and listen to exactly what Chris had said. I wanted to see if I could break these down individually outside of the pressure of him being in the room and needing answers immediately. My job here was to be the professional, which often meant focusing on controlling my reactions when things seem to be going a thousand miles per minute and going back in with a calm head to sort out the pieces later. It's a good practice for me and sets a good example for my clients.

In listening to the recordings of Chris, one line in particular jumped out at me.

"You're trying to tell me that three major failures in four years is not that big of a deal…That I'm not some embarrassment, a joke in the community…"

He seemed to be baiting me into an argument. The feelings of being laughed at or ridiculed were his fight or flight system being activated. His brain was looking to confirm his underlying fears. Behind this question, however, were some realities he was dealing with, and that is where it was important that I stay focused.

I had heard similar statements from other clients. If they didn't stay with an employer for more than five years they felt guilty. They assumed they were supposed to stay for much longer or people were going to look down on them for changing jobs. Their definition of success was tied to tenure.

The reality is that the median tenure for the average worker is between three to four years and has been since the mid-90s. The idea of working for the same company for more than ten years is now what happens to outliers, and is far from the norm. The reasons for this number have less to do with people being disloyal or uncommitted as much as they are about fewer opportunities to advance, less in incentives and raises, and the instability of businesses themselves. The ability to find a job and retire in 40 years with a pension has been all but nonexistent for close to forty years. But that's not the story they were taught, it is counter to the definition of success they had learned, and it was creating feelings of guilt, lack, and insecurity for many people.

In my approach with clients, I focused a lot on finding places where they could be consistent in creating success. I relied on finding platforms for my clients that matched the goals they were trying to achieve. Was I indirectly selling them on that longevity? Reinforcing a definition of success that no longer existed? Could I actually have been making their struggle worse? The research made me realize how I reinforced the very narrative they were struggling to figure out. No wonder they were getting defensive.

As I continued to research, I found that 20 percent of the jobs people have today did not exist 15 years ago. One-fifth of the workforce is employed in a job that they could never have prepared for in high school because it had not yet been imagined yet. How do you get consistency when things are changing so quickly? I had never considered the need to prepare people for jobs that didn't even exist.

In performance consulting outside of work and business, the direction is pretty straightforward. You figure out the objective: a race to win, a team to beat, a speed to achieve, or a distance to cover. When you have this figured out, you just work backward. You build out the plan, measure the progress weekly, follow the steps that people had figured out before, and then the difference is who puts in the most work.

But if you don't know what you will be doing in five years, perhaps because the job does not exist, this model can easily become a recipe for frustration. I had been pushing my clients into these old models consistently. I focused so many people on getting the secure position or following the proven route, when many of them would need to learn how to create entirely new routes to create success. Maybe the security I was looking to create was my own, because it sure didn't seem like I was creating it for my clients.

If I was worried I was doing more harm than good before, then these discoveries were not helping. What did I need to change to help people prepare for this constantly changing nature of work? If I was so convinced of the importance of security, how could I help them create it when they could no longer count on a job to do it for them?

The research was creating more questions than answers, but I had to keep going. I listened through our recorded sessions and more issues came into view.

One of these "three major failures" Chris talked about was his business. As I listened, it was like I hadn't heard the conversation before, like I had missed obvious statements that were right in front of me, as if he had been trying to open my eyes the entire time.

"Look at me! I'm a dream manager who can't achieve his own dreams. I was a motivational speaker and now the only thing I am motivated to do is drink beer and crawl in a hole..." "Failure" was a word he'd used many times since he closed down his business and walked away with the heavy debt load.

In a fixed state, classic definition of failure, he was right. If the only thing that defined success or failure was his financial success in this singular endeavor, then a failure he was. Compared to the majority of small business owners, however, he was average. He had been in business for about three years. The average lifespan of a small business is closer to two years. Are all of these people failures? I would argue no.

But getting this across to a client like Chris was a whole other ball of wax. Just as we have been taught that we're only going to have one or two jobs throughout our lifetime, despite the evidence to the contrary, we also seem to be under the assumption that businesses are all going to succeed. We get so focused on the outcome that we miss all of the potential validation along the way. There was so much he had learned in the past three years, so much that could prepare him for the future, but his current definitions were making it hard to see. Our focus was blinding him to his own potential.

I had to question whether I'd prepared Chris for a broader definition of success from the beginning. My training, everything that had made me successful as a consultant before, had gotten me hyper-focused on a singular definition of success. A definition that required both security and validation to be available in ways that seemed less and less available today.

What if all his experiences could provide the kind of validation that would help him continue to move forward? What if he could provide his own security? What if there was a different, more complete, definition of success that would allow my clients to navigate this ever-changing world? There had to be.

In the midst of what felt like failure after failure for Chris, there was a place where he had been quite successful. To be honest, I didn't pay much attention to this until I saw how badly not running had affected him in our recent discussion. "And now that I tore my Achilles, I can't even go for a run to blow off steam. In fact, I may never run again. At least I was successful at that." It's the last part of that statement I couldn't get over…"at least I was successful at that."

I knew running was a great source of validation for him. It

gave him a sense of control, seemed to reinforce his behavior just by doing it, and even gave him outside recognition. All of which were key elements of good validation, things that reinforce behavior and keep people moving forward. What I hadn't realized was how similar his running journey actually was to his professional journey.

Chris's approach to running was as disjointed as his approach to his professional life had been. Every time he completed a distance, he would try something new. When he didn't like triathlons or fell short of goals, he quit and moved on. What started as speed training for half marathons, complete with heart-rate monitors, journals, training plans, and custom clothing, had transformed into not even carrying a watch, not following a training plan, and running completely by feel.

This change allowed him to run a hundred miles. The failures he had had along the way, not finishing races, injuries, even the painful training runs, were all things that had actually made him more prepared for the 100 mile race he had recently completed. Changes, challenges, and failures had seemed to hold him back professionally, but were the very thing that prepared him for success in running. They allowed him to figure out what kind of runner he wanted to be and focus only on the kind of running he was best suited to do.

He was not alone in this experience either. In 1994 there were four million runners in the US, and in 2013, more than 18 million. While on the surface, this could simply look like really good marketing by the running industry, what I couldn't get over was how, in a time when so many businesses were struggling with employee engagement, people were actively paying to be engaged in the work of running.

Very, very few people were actually getting paid to run. Arguably less than one percent and even they weren't being paid very well. And, yet, more and more people were spending their hard-earned money to do something they could easily do for free.

While I didn't immediately know what to do with this information, for my own practice, it was enormously helpful. Running provided people with validation and a sense of control (security) by providing an activity that was predictable and had a progression that could build their confidence. More importantly, runners had a different definition of success.

To me, this meant the internal rules hadn't changed. People still, inherently, needed validation and security. And, because they weren't getting it at work, they were finding it in other activities. From marathons and half marathons to Spartan Races and Tough Mudders, from triathlons to any other number of competitions in and outside of running, people turned to these activities for the validation and security they used to get at work.

The question for me, for Chris, for the rest of my clients, and perhaps for the working world, is how could we get this same reward from the daily work that we do? How do we take an environment that seems to have lost so much of its predictability and still find the security that is so vital? When things can change so rapidly, and the goalposts move without any notice, how can we create the kind of validation that will allow us to keep moving forward, keep striving, and keep believing in ourselves? How can we play by the rules when the rules keep changing?

"I don't know what to do." "I'm not sure who I am anymore." These were the thoughts filling Chris's mind with fear and doubt. He had redefined himself so many times he didn't know who he was anymore. He was quickly losing his ability to dream, to hope for the future, and to believe in his power to rise to the next challenge.

Although I still had no solution in mind, I felt I at least had a better understanding of the problem now. If I could share this with Chris, perhaps I could get him to look at his challenges from a different angle. I too, was going to have to change my approach, my expectations, and some of the underlying assumptions. It wasn't going to be easy.

I was convinced the game had changed. Something I think we'd all known for some time. But I had a client in crisis and I knew the insights wouldn't be enough to solve his problem. I just hoped it would keep him from giving up on a solution.

9
THE CEILING

There are times in my work when a client session takes every bit of skill I've got. Given our last interaction, I knew my focus and intention had to be at their absolute peak. While all days are important, this day, this interaction, feels especially full of potential. This day could make or break the relationship. He was giving me one more shot and I wanted to give him the best chance.

This was the one extra meeting Chris had granted me. He didn't see much value in continuing on with the consulting relationship, something that reflected his current mindset as much as it did my own struggles as a professional.

I was ready. I had done my research. I had a list of things to work on that might engage him again, and I was open to trying a few new things out myself. I would meet him half-way.

I knew it was likely that my client's limbic system would be on high alert, putting him at the threshold of fight or flight. And mine, too. My brain was not immune to these responses. I can take these things too personally, especially with Chris, and I had to watch my own emotional regulation.

Once we get into fight or flight, we diminish the potential for any growth or movement. Defensive stances keep us from forward motion. Our brain's executive system, the place we need to envision those positive changes, shuts down when the limbic is overactive.

It's up to me, the professional, to give us both the best possible chance at finding a new direction. I feel the weight on my shoulders. Here goes. Wish me luck.

"How have you been, Chris?"

"Not good."

He isn't going to waste any time. "What are you feeling?" I ask hesitantly.

"I can feel my head in the pillow but I can't get myself to lift it up. I'm not tired; my eyes are wide open. But my head stays here for hours, thinking, pondering, looking for a reason to get out of bed."

Hmmm. Sounds like he just needs to get the underlying frustration off his chest first. Security and validation are at work during these coaching sessions as much as any other time. He needs to be heard and validated so he can work himself into feeling secure. There's never an exact way to get this done, so I'll try to let him lead as much as I am able.

"Sounds rough, man."

"The latest I ever used to sleep in might be seven or eight in the morning, and now I hardly get out before ten. I always thought it was just because I was a morning person. Now I'm coming to realize that it was more about having something to do, something I cared about doing. And now, I just don't feel as though I have anything to do that matters."

I want to interject and help him solve the problem, but I need to wait for the right time. Whenever he presents a problem, something it seems obvious I can help with, it triggers my own need for validation. But that's about me, not him. So

I invite him to go on.

"Tell me more about this. I'm here to listen."

"It's like I'm not even needed at work. I'm just waiting for the merger to happen. Some people are telling me this is the perfect job, getting paid to do very little, but I hate it a little more every day. It's like I'm a ghost walking through my day. I could be there or not be there and it would make no difference. No one would notice and no one would care."

He's just expressing here, I have to remind myself, just exercising the emotions. I try to stay out of the way.

"Every morning I stare at the ceiling. There are these shadows from uneven paint. But, in staring at them so long, they become entire worlds I could play in, get lost in, lose my mind in. I just stare off into them and imagine a better life. One where I'm not just a screw up."

This is his brain being overactive. Just the stream of consciousness that attempts to ease that pain. I'm going to encourage him to go all the way through it. Maybe we can use it, or at least expressing it might allow him to be open to moving forward.

"When you do get up, what are you doing?" I ask tentatively.

"I'm told I should get out of the house and meet people. But I don't want to meet anyone. I don't want to talk with anyone, I don't want to tell people my story, I don't want to tell them what I do, I hate my job, I hate sitting around and not being able to run, and I just don't care to look for another job. To set up for another failure."

"You've been through a lot, Chris. The changes at work and your torn Achilles. Processing these emotions is the right thing to do. You know that feeling bad for a while is to be expected."

He is human, after all.

"This is happening more and more often now. Once I start thinking about something, even simply leaving the house, things begin to spiral. Everything comes at once. I should never have taken this job in the first place. Without having running, it's not bearable anymore. Going to work feels like I have been defeated by my worst rival and, as punishment, I am forced to go to his house and wash his socks. Every. Single. Day."

Despite myself, I have to smile at the colorful simile. Chris' spirit is not completely extinguished. And now we're moving toward the source of pain. This feels like the part that needs to be heard and validated. We'll start here and move forward, slowly.

"It sounds like you're tired of being in this situation. Where do you want to go from here?"

"I want to be motivated again. I want to find a reason to get out of this bed and start the day early again. But right now I just don't care. I'm not interested in getting my hopes up to let myself down again. I just want to leave. To go somewhere that I can't be a burden to my wife anymore, to the rest of the world anymore, so this pathetic story of my shortcomings does not continue to leave such a path of destruction anymore."

Despite how bleak it sounds, he just opened the door, if only a crack. I can feel him relax just a hair. He's still engaged, slightly less afraid and less defensive. He opened up enough to gain access to the part of his brain that we both need. Perhaps only for a short time, but that's often all we need.

"Chris, there are some things I've been researching that I think will interest you. Some interesting changes in the economy and in the nature of work itself are in play here. If we shift how we look at things and define them, you'll see you're doing better than you think."

"Sounds like putting chocolate on a piece of crap," he

says, shaking his head.

I expected some mild pushback, but that doesn't make it any less frustrating. I have to watch myself to keep from getting defensive. It feels like time to push a bit. He is challenging me and I take that as a sign that he's ready to be challenged in turn.

"I know, somewhere inside, you still want to be successful, Chris. I know that despite the setbacks you know you can still do great things. I know you believe in your own potential."

"You don't know a damn thing about what I believe."

Uh-oh. His face goes tight and I can feel anger and fear rushing back in.

"What the hell good is being successful if I'm miserable? If I'm working all the time and never home? If I'm so angry all the time and no one wants to be around me?"

Dammit. There it is again. He shows a moment of hopefulness only to cycle back into hyper focus on defeat.

I can feel my own mind start to get noisy again. How the hell do I pull him back? I want to be angry at him. I watch as the comments I want to say flash through my mind:

"You're making yourself miserable!"

But he knew that.

"These ridiculous thoughts are killing you!"

But I had to find a way for him to want to feel alive again.

None of those are constructive, regardless of whether or not they were true. It's just my own limbic system taking over, and I'm the professional, so I pause, I breathe, and I think of something better. Get under this statement, find out what's behind it. That's where the work begins.

Deep breath. "Okay, if it's not about you achieving, being successful, hitting your own goals, what do you think it's about, Chris? I'm really trying to help you here, man. We're on the same side, but I need you to meet me halfway."

"Really? If you are so keen on helping me, why haven't you asked me?"

"Asked you what?" Now I'm confused.

"What's important to me. You talk all the time about being successful, but you've never asked me what's important about success, or money, or business, or even having a job, to ME! You know how important that question is, you've seen me ask it of others, but every time I come here and watch you assume you know the answer it just makes me feel like you aren't listening. Like you don't even care about anything but having me appear successful so you look successful."

I sit there like a deer in the headlights. Every part of me wants to fire back a ready answer: "Of course I've asked you," or "I know you well enough I don't need to ask." Anything that would hide the obvious truth of his statement. He is absolutely right. I'd never asked him, and I wasn't asking any of my clients.

I am too stunned to respond.

"What if I don't really care about money? What if success, status, the right title or driving the cool car doesn't actually mean anything to me? Would we still be doing the same things? Would I have gone through all of this crap? It feels like I've been working real hard to earn something I don't even want. And I have no motivation, energy, or emotional reserves left to try and do it again."

I swallow hard, take a deep breath, and offer a response. No more defending.

"I guess I just thought I knew you well enough. We've talked about being successful in business and in your running. You know I focus on performance, Chris. It was the performance in the jobs and activities you were currently pursuing that I focused on. I'm not sure what else you want from me."

Now I'm just trying to keep him on board.

"You're always trying to separate the professional side from the personal side. Like one doesn't directly affect the other. Like we can even separate them anymore. These failures have all hurt me as personally as they have professionally. My marriage isn't the same, my friendships aren't the same, and I don't even have the same image of myself anymore."

I nod in stunned agreement, too surprised to say anything.

"I'm no longer interested in working with you if it's not going to be personal. I'm asking you to make this about me."

I feel a burst of anger. The ultimatum pulls me out of my silent state and forces a reaction.

"How was this not about you? It's always been about you. About finding the job or business that will give you security. About finding processes that will help you be successful in those positions, in running, or anything else."

"That's just the thing, I think the last years have proven I'm not going to find security in some job that someone else gives me, I can't even find security in a job I create for myself. Can you really guarantee that it can?

Wait, this was the connection I was trying to make for him. He stole my thunder. I've been so busy being defensive that I missed the fact that we're actually on the same page. Things suddenly seem to slow down.

Chris stands and says, "I don't know what information you say you have, what new strategy or perspective you are working on, but if it's just about being successful for the sake of success, about some white picket fence dream, or any other assumed approach, I'm not interested. I'm going to go to the bathroom and make a phone call to give you a second, and we can reschedule if we need, I just need you to know, if we are going to keep working together, things have to change."

I take a deep breath before responding.

"I agree, let's take a break. When you come back, we can figure it out together."

Sometimes you're the windshield, sometimes you're the bug. These shortcomings on my end are suddenly so painfully obvious. I'm questioning everything right now, including my own professional worth. I've been focused singularly on being a consultant, on having the answers, giving advice, following a certain plan. He was asking me to be a coach.

I have 15 minutes to figure out my next move. This isn't normal, stopping a session mid-stream. And yet, giving us both time to reset seems right.

I'm not sure who's running the session anymore.

I'm supposed to be the one who understands the importance of security. I know how it plays out in the brain, how it can change behavior, and how it can lead a guy like Chris to exactly the dark place he's been. But now Chris is showing me, the supposed professional, how complicit I've been in creating that very hell.

I stare at the papers I brought, spread out on the table as if providing a buffer between us. They are supposed to help us find the answers he's looking for and enable us to find better strategies and solutions. But as I ponder what Chris said about security, I realize it was not an answer he was looking for, but a better question.

My experience tells me this current discomfort is the best thing Chris could hope for. Some people wait their entire life to get hit with the realities that are now giving him the opportunity, perhaps forcing him, to define his own value.

I too am uncomfortable right now. My entire professional approach has been challenged. I'm supposed to be the guy who knows the answers for my clients. But that's clearly not enough for Chris. He's asking me to give up control, to engage in questions to which I have no answer, to join him on a journey where neither of us know the destination. This showdown feels as though my own security is being pulled right out from under me.

I feel sick. Maybe I should feel ill, or worse. If my clients are struggling with this, I need to struggle too. It feels like Chris and I are hitting rock bottom at the same time. If I'm asking him to grow, I have to be ready to do the same.

If the social contract between businesses and their employees, and between entrepreneurs and the market, has changed so drastically in recent years, maybe it's time the consultant-client relationship changed too. If everything else is changing, if we can't count on the outside anymore, it makes perfect sense to focus on the inside.

These feelings Chris and my clients have communicated are ones I've been trying to ignore myself. I'm that college kid that got the grades, got the degree, got the job, and gets home every night wondering if this is it. We define ourselves through the degree, the school and the job, like characters in a book we're no longer interested in reading. Entire lives spent exploring a game someone else created, maps someone else designed, an illusion of happiness seen on billboards and commercials. All these paths that promised a pot of gold, forgetting that all along we ourselves hold all the treasure we need for fulfillment.

If the roadmaps we used to rely on were changing, maybe my job was really to help create new ones, not attempt to rebuild something that no longer exists.

I could see the fortune in our current misfortune. This pain is the gift. This inability to see was a blank slate. These failures were signposts. Chris and I had a chance to rewrite our entire script and change our futures together.

I'm seeing a glimmer of the real potential: to make this about the people themselves, their own definition of success. To focus on their hopes and dreams, on who they really are. On their true value.

This, right now, has to be about the deepest needs Chris can identify. Anything we've dodged before must come to light. It's likely to be uncomfortable, even a bit more personal than I'm used to exploring. Maybe that's what I've avoided for so long.

Chris is here now. We look each other in the eye. It's his turn to talk now. I just have to find a way to trust the process.

"You're right, Chris." I say, swallowing my pride whole. "You're absolutely right about this needing to be more about you. I do have some things to share, but they can wait. If you're ready, let's start here."

"I'm ready," he says, sitting up and taking a big breath. "Go ahead."

I have no idea if this will work or not. No sense of where this conversation might lead. I think I know the questions I'll ask, but where it goes will be up to him. I'm giving up control. It feels uncomfortable and natural at the same time.

"What's important about being successful to you?" My back straightens. It feels right. Like something I should have asked years ago.

"Actually, I've never really cared about being successful. Even those times when I sold the accounts or crossed the finish line at some race, it was never really about success."

This feels new, less forced, and kind of exciting.

"Then what do you think it was? What's important about achieving things to you?"

"I think it has more to do with what I get to see in other people. When I finish a race, and people ask about it, I can always see them dreaming of their own goals. It almost always turns into them asking me if I think they could do this race or that race. And, at work, it was always about how excited everyone else got when I sold an account. My boss, the other people, I could see this helping them toward their own dreams."

"So it sounds like it's about helping others with their dreams and their own goals. Why do you think that's so important to you?" Reflect back and keep the momentum going.

"I've just seen the opposite so many times. It's those moments when you see someone stop believing in their own dreams. I've seen it in people I care very much about. I can even spot it in the eyes of people I've never met before. It's that look, like you know they don't believe in themselves any more, don't think they have any power, or purpose, or beauty, and it absolutely breaks my heart, man. What's most important to me is helping people believe again. I want to feel like I'm making an impact on a person's ability to hope again."

I am blown away. I need to keep going.

"What causes that low point?"

"It's hard to put that into words. I just know I've felt myself heading there before. I think I've been real close lately. And, when the feeling comes, it can be all-encompassing, like a weight I can't remove. I felt it when I was a kid. I saw members of my family go through it."

"So what is the opposite of that feeling? What chases that darkness away?"

"Freedom." He pauses. "The sense that I'm in control of my own destiny, that I have choice in my situation, that I can influence the outcome. It's absolutely essential that I am the captain of the ship and not a bobber in the ocean. Nothing is more important. If anything really matters about success to me, it's helping people feel like they have some control over their destiny. I want them to know their power, to believe they have a choice, to know the feeling freedom can create within themselves. I think that starts with believing I can do the same for myself."

Chris and I are both quiet for a moment, I feel myself trembling, nervous. I was humbled by seeing Chris in a way I had never seen him before and anxious about being able to deliver what he needed. Then I step into it.

"I finally understand," I say. "Now everything we do will be about that freedom. You have my word."

10
REWRITING THE PAST

Freedom?

What did that mean?

Seriously, the idea sounded awesome, inspiring even. It also sounded like living out in the wilderness in a tent.

Trust the process they say. I hope it works too, because it's the only thing I could do during our discussion as I really had no idea how to even begin to make freedom tangible. It was just an idea floating in the air, and if I was going to be able to help him I would need to make it measurable.

Chris has this philosophy of Educo. To bring forth, to extract from. I'm not sure if I actually buy into the notion or if I'm just out of options. Maybe he knows exactly what he needs to do, and I just need to get out of his way. Following Educo meant pulling what we would need out of him, my job would be to stay focused on the questions.

Our latest conversation could have gone any direction. I was worried about Chris spiraling deeper, and I was worried about losing control of the dialogue. But for the first time, a door had opened. Suddenly this felt more like a partnership than a teacher-student interaction. Maybe I needed him to be a part of the process as much as he needed me.

My own ego was tied up in trying to have the next right answer for him. But as I kept on trying to connect my strategies with his ideas of freedom, I came up empty. Maybe in this existential crisis he needed someone beyond me, perhaps a shaman or a priest.

As Mike Tyson said: "Everyone has a plan, until they get punched in the face." The economy was changing, we both knew that. What we didn't know was how to respond to it.

The idea of the plan coming from within seemed like the only thing that made sense. If the outside world wasn't giving us a plan anymore, we'd have to find it ourselves. Educo, at this point, seemed to be about necessity as much as opportunity. We decided to start the process with his resume.

"Let me see that thing."

Resumes were my bread and butter. I can see, almost at a glance, exactly how to position someone for that next job or promotion. A bit of an outdated skill, I was fast realizing.

"What should I do?" Chris asks, almost habitually.

"Well, let's start with…" The words seem to come out of my mouth automatically, like being caught in a trap and just realizing it. I set the resume down.

"What are you doing?" Chris seems startled.

Truth be told, I'm not sure what I'm doing. Only that I feel the sensation of sameness, like Chris and I are repeating a familiar but flawed pattern. Right now, the little voice inside my own head wants me to change course.

"Look, Chris. Here's the deal. I promised you all our work would go toward helping you create freedom. I don't know what that means or how we do it, I'll admit. All I know is that we have to change our approach to everything, starting with this resume."

It feels like a gamble. Chris doesn't have time to mess around with some experimental approach to job seeking. He's going to be without work soon, and both of us feel that pressure. But I know I don't want him sitting here the rest of our lives, having the same conversation. So, again, I trust the process.

"How do you suggest we do that?" Chris asks the logical question.

"I really have no idea." Where I'd been holding thoughts inside, with this new partnership approach, I express them out loud. "I've done plenty of work with businesses on creating a vision or a mission. Maybe we can apply that here."

"Okay."

"What's the purpose of this resume?" Let's question the obvious, try not to let assumptions get in the way.

"To get a job."

"I get that. It's a device to be employed again. But, if freedom is really what you want, where's the freedom in this resume?"

"I'm not sure what you're talking about. Freedom's nowhere to be found in my resume."

"Why not?"

"Because a resume is for an employer. They don't care what freedom means to me."

Now we are rolling.

"Ok, sure. Maybe this resume is built for an employer. Maybe that's the problem. If freedom is so important, why isn't your resume built for you?"

"What would I put in that?" I feel a hint of engagement from him as I'm warming to the subject, too.

"You would put all of the accomplishments you are proud of, you would list all of the skills and talents you have that are engaging and inspiring to you, the things you have done that made you feel most alive." Wow, that feels good. I find myself talking with my hands, painting a picture, it was quickly turning into one of the most exciting interactions I'd had in a long time. "You know, when you actually felt like you were creating the freedom that you say is important to you."

"That actually sounds kind of cool." I see a ghost of a smile, and it's a beautiful thing.

"And it should. Freedom is your value, Chris. And, because it's such a high value for you, it makes sense that you've found it, in some ways, in the past. More importantly, if we're going to have any chance of making it in the future, knowing where you've created it before is important."

My voice is calming now. The stage has been set.

"I think I know what you mean. It's like creating a resume just for me. A couple pages devoted to who I really am, what I really care about, am proud about, and the things I do well that I would actually want to do again. Is that right?"

"That's it!"

"What if it doesn't match up with any jobs that are out there?" He tosses out a last-ditch effort to ease his own unease.

"Valid point, Chris. But what if it does? More importantly, is it worth doing even if it doesn't directly lead to a job?"

"Absolutely!"

I left that meeting on top of the world. Somewhere, in the middle of our conversation, I had a distinct realization. If a person spends so much of their life at their job, then it absolutely has to be connected, in some way, to things most important to them. Being able to feel as though he created freedom, if he acknowledged it, could potentially be a great source of validation for him. If freedom was important to Chris, there had to be remnants of it in his past that we could use.

The data I wanted to share with him before, about the changing economy and changing nature of work, were still important pieces of information. But it also felt useless to share with him at this time. There was nothing he could do about it. Things were changing and he knew it, the numbers just made it more formal.

I've always considered myself a coach. At least I'd always used that term. But this was the first time I actually felt like one. Something was different about this conversation. It was less forced, and there was less pressure on me to come up with an answer.

I could provide some insight but it was more like encouraging exploration than it was sharing my expertise. The expertise just helped me know where to focus, where to dig deeper. Our conversation had been more about getting him focused than giving him the answers. Freedom would provide the focus, the validation he was struggling to find in his personal and professional life.

Chris and I had been guilty of chasing the short-term fix, and in doing so, we'd only made the real problems even harder to solve. When Chris' short-term need was financial, we got him certified to sell products. We answered the problem but distracted him from what was really important. When he lost his job, instead of focusing on what so obviously engaged him, we took the closest, easiest job we could find, tried to be someone else so we could feel accepted, and put any idea of security into the hands of an employer or the market and removing it from his control. With each change, his belief that it was available diminished.

But this time, I was determined not to take the easy way out. If I was really going to be a good coach, it was my job to identify his power, help him see through the fear and remind him of the incredible value he's already created. Deep down, it was exactly the kind of coach I'd wanted to be the whole time. I realized I'd been pretending to have the answer because my ego was scared, and I was trying to convince the clients of my value.

Our job now? Get him to believe in his own power to creating security himself. To do this we would have to find a way to validate his value. To connect his success to his potential.

It all sounds easy on paper: Focus on what you really want and get in touch with the things you really enjoy or do well. But in my next conversation with Chris, I began to realize how much work we really had to do. It turns out that going deeper takes courage—a lot of courage.

"I've been working on this resume all week. It's crazy how much stuff wasn't on the original version."

"Well Chris, you changed where you were pointing the flashlight. When the bright light is on what you think you need right now, the beam doesn't reach very far. You were bound to find something you missed before."

He offers a half-hearted smile. "It's inspiring to think I can focus more on this freedom thing. But now I'm worried again. Like, it's good to know this stuff, but I can't see how I can put that into a job or any kind of a living."

"Chris, I know the job is important, and it should be. At the same time, you told me that you wanted our work together to be about freedom."

"Yes, but how is patting myself on the back going to create freedom? And, what kind of freedom do I have if I can't find a job? I've been sending tons of resumes out and nobody's answering."

His shoulders fall. The wolf peeks his head back in the door. We need to dive deeper.

"Tell me, why did you choose the stuff you did? On this

resume, you show a specific event as a teacher where you made an impact on a kid's life. You have a time when someone came up and told you about a change in their life based on something they'd heard from you. And you include running your first marathon. What do all these have in common?"

"I guess those are the moments I felt like what I did had some purpose. Maybe it even had an impact on others. These are the places I thought I really brought my talents."

"But why? Why do you feel that way?"

"I'm not sure what you mean."

"You could have written any number of things here, Chris: your graduate degree, the bigger races you've run, or the money you made in certain situations. But you didn't. You focused on where you made an impact on others."

"I guess I did."

"Tell me why? Why are these things so engaging for you?" I'm pushing hard now.

There's a long pause. Not of frustration, but internal dialogue. He's conjuring up the courage to say out loud something he's never fully admitted, even to himself.

He exhales and begins speaking deliberately, looking at the floor. "So the thing is, I was abused when I was a kid. It was both physical and emotional abuse, but, most of all, I guess it left me feeling powerless. I spent a lot of my younger years not believing I could do much. The things I did do, I did because I was scared. When I finally found high school football, it became a chance to prove myself, and to hit back at the world through physical effort. I loved to play, but I knew I didn't have the talent to ever be any good. I remember being out on the football field after summer practice. My coach brought us around in a circle and asked what position we planned on playing that coming year. As each of my teammates made bold statements like 'I'm going to be quarter-back' or 'I'm playing linebacker' I began feeling out of place. By the time they got to me, I was so afraid I just shrugged my shoulders. That coach was having none of it. I remember every word he said to me in that moment: 'Chris, you're one of the hardest-working people out on this field. You're here for this extra practice when most of the team is at home. You do this week in and week out. Now, you might not believe me now, but I want you to hear me clearly: WITH YOUR WORK ETHIC, YOU CAN HAVE ANY POSITION YOU WANT ON THIS FIELD.'"

As he tells the story, Chris straightens his shoulders. His chin lifts and his chest swells.

"That one interaction changed the way I looked at everything. I didn't really believe him at first, but I decided to try and believe it. I did get the position I wanted on the team and, for the first time, really started to believe in what I could possibly deliver. I had to prove him right, and I did the work necessary to do it. As my confidence grew, it was like breaking out of a prison."

Incredible. This is our moment of discovery. Helping him make the next connection felt natural.

"Freedom. It was freedom, right Chris? He helped to develop the thing you value the most today."

"It was. But that's not the end of the story. Ten years later, I found that coach again. I asked if he knew what an impact he had on my life. But he didn't remember the pep talk. This one event that changed my life forever, he didn't even remember."

Chris shrugs and shakes his head. I can't tell if he's sad or angry, or both.

"I was shocked. I didn't know how to take it. How could something so powerful for me have been not even memorable to him? Initially, I couldn't make sense of it."

I realize that him not remembering was every bit as powerful as the initial pep talk. I am a bit confused, so I dig deeper. "I'm not sure what you mean?"

"If he didn't remember the interaction, it meant that such a profound impact happened by accident. The freedom I found that day was as random as someone losing their keys."

His eyes are big now. His face is fully engaged.

"I don't get, it Chris." I wonder if I'd taken him down the wrong road.

"The reason those things I wrote in the resume were so important is that I did them on purpose. If my football coach could have that much impact on me accidentally, then imagine what an impact I could have if I chose to make my actions have an impact on purpose."

He's speaking now with a strength I hadn't heard before.

"What impact is that, Chris?" I want to hear him to say it out loud again.

"Freedom. The same thing I want. Helping other people find it is vitally important to me. It's what drove me as a teacher. It's the time I made a difference as a speaker. And what mattered in that marathon wasn't covering some distance, but the look in this one kid's eyes when he saw me crossing the finish line. I could tell he was dreaming. I could tell he saw himself in me. All these times, I now see I was just trying to help someone else realize their own potential for freedom."

He is unearthing the validation he had received all along. Only now he i connecting it with what he cared about, things within his control. Identifying where he had already created it, almost instantaneously growing the belief he can do it again right in front of my eyes. He speaks as if opening his eyes for the first time and describing the color of the sky.

"So, what it sounds like, what you really do best, is giving people the same freedom that is important to you? When you are delivering the most value, you are delivering freedom."

The connection is strong now. Without even so much as a prompt, he goes deeper.

He looks down and takes a deep breath. "The person who took freedom from me didn't remember either."

"You mean the person who abused you?" I ask slowly.

"I confronted them, years later, and they didn't even remember what they did. Like they were sick or something. Like this big, scary, impactful thing to me was just some accident for someone else that didn't even make it on their radar."

There is anger and confusion in his voice.

"Then we take that understanding and use it going forward. No more accidents. Whatever it is you decide to do; a job, a business, or anything else, it has to be about helping people create freedom on purpose. Right?"

"Yes. Yes! Too much of the last few years have happened by accident. That stops now. Let's do this thing on purpose."

That voice had no confusion at all. Freedom was the value he delivered, what he could now use to identify points of validation. It was the positive tool he had acquired in the midst of a negative event. An idea that was becoming clearer with each discussion.

What we choose to take from our past, how we make sense of the events, becomes our story. When we finally looked into Chris' story deeply enough, clarifying what it meant and what it could mean, it seemed to open the door to a potential future, and past, that had before been hidden in the recesses of his mind. Success could be something much more meaningful to him. There was no external reward that could possibly compete with his biggest longing: Freedom created on purpose.

Although the path forward was still unknown, we had a better idea of the places that we would see along the way. Neither of us knew where it would go. But now we knew full well what we both wanted to create, together.

.

11
FINDING VALUE

Chris was opening my eyes to things that should have been obvious. What really inspired him was unique to him, as it was to each one of my clients. What was consistent across the board is that they had found it before. All the motivation needed to begin was available in their past if they looked hard enough. It was the seed we could begin to water.

In my attempts to help people as a coach, I had often neglected the power of their past experiences. We spent so much time trying to figure out what to do next that we lost all the momentum we had before.

I'd noticed that in times of transition people wanted an entirely new plan. They wanted the new magic recipe. And it almost never worked. Any plan without a foundation built on past success was doomed to collapse. I could see how vital it was to connect with those strengths, skills and tools from the past, rather than ignoring them in search of something new.

Chris was diving deeper too, and connecting to past strengths. I could see him looking beyond the temporary pain of the moment, and remembering the things that engaged him and the places he had been successful on his own terms.

There were glimmers of the value he could deliver when he was focused on creating freedom.

In the new economy, this is how we find our own freedom. We must be able to see through the clouds of doubt and fear and understand the battle between the stronger and weaker parts of the brain: the limbic system trying to protect us and the pre-frontal cortex attempting to bring reason, imagination, and hope into the equation. The limbic system is always stronger, but if you can continue to actively look past the initial fear, you give the pre-frontal system a chance.

Our brains are designed for protection, which works great when running from bears or jumping out of the way of an oncoming car. But in an environment where survival requires ingenuity, imagination, and complex reasoning, the less powerful part of our brain becomes the most important. It's our true keeper of security. By recalling the best of our past, we can purposefully re-ignite the pre-frontal cortex, shifting from fear and protection to confidence and creation.

This became so much more of my focus with clients. Instead of offering the quick fix to relieve their pain, I reconnected them to the confidence they once knew.

"Where have you felt most alive?" It was one of my favorite questions. Or, "tell me about a time when you were proud of yourself."

Better yet: "Was there ever a time in your life you knew you were firing on all cylinders, bringing your best, or feeling as though what you were doing really mattered?"

These questions changed me as a coach. No longer did I have to feel like I had to solve everything. And clients responded differently when I wasn't telling them what to do. They may have been coming to me for answers, but deep down they knew they had them the entire time. They were coming to me for permission.

Where I was at my best was in building confidence instead

of providing solutions. It was breaking a cycle instead of perpetuating a process that got them stuck in the first place. The answer to these uncertain economic times, it seemed, was less about escaping through some temporary solution and more about navigating with an internal confidence. Chris had given me a powerful tool, and now I felt guilty for not having used it before.

As helpful as the process was, however, it was only part of what would ultimately be needed. Like the passing streak of a New Year's resolution, the insights got people excited and ready to move forward. But the realities of life and perpetual feelings of doubt are formidable opponents.

Eventually, Chris hit a plateau. Only this time, instead of frantically searching for a solution, we chose to look at it as another opportunity. When he walked in the door, it was obvious the momentum was wearing off. The signs of confidence in his body and engagement in his language were losing their vibrant tone.

"How are you feeling, Chris?" I ask gently.

He looks up, as if reminded he was supposed to be feeling better and not wanting to take that away from me.

"I feel good," he says, trying to put on his happy face.

"Really? You feel good? You don't really look like you feel good. Something has to be on your mind." I want to give him permission to talk.

"I feel like I had a great experience a couple weeks ago, like our conversation really opened some things up for me, but it's feeling harder and harder to hold onto each day."

I can tell he's hiding his own emotional state, and I need to keep mine in check. I've got to work harder to make it about him, letting him know I will be ok. Momentum is important in the tenuous position Chris finds himself, and it's even more important that the momentum is authentic. We can't hide anything.

"I understand," I say. "It's like you come home from some weekend workshop or conference full of excitement, only to be brought back down to what feels like reality in a short couple of weeks."

"I want to believe I can create all this, but every time I go out into the world, it's like the voice comes back. I'm constantly reminded of my prior failures, of all the times I tried and came up short." His head drops a little again like he's done something wrong.

"What do you mean, 'when you go out in the world'?" I ask.

"When I look for a job, when I talk to people about what I should do next, when I simply think about how far removed I feel from any real sense of freedom today."

The way he says it sounds like he's staggering under an enormous weight. Every part of me wants to answer this for him. I want to tell Chris that he's good enough and to go find things that he can do. I want to outline for him where I think he has freedom, how close I think he is to where I believe, with all my professional expertise, he should be. But I'm using his Educo process now, and I'm trying my best to trust he has the answers within himself.

"So you can see where you have had freedom in the past, but can't see where it is today?" I ask. "Do you not think it's available or is it simply not as important as we'd discussed?" I want him to be clear about the problem.

"I absolutely believe it's important. What I'm struggling to figure out is how I can create freedom and make money. I have to have a job. I have to pay the bills. I have responsibilities. I can't just run out and be magically free because of one conversation."

"Let's be clear here, Chris. You do want this, right?"

"Yes, I want it. I just don't know how to keep the momentum going. I feel like it's available in these brief moments, and the next moment it's gone. Like I'm on top of the world for a second, only to be convinced that nothing will get better the next."

As he talks, I know I have plenty of strategies to help him. I could show that it is about controlling his focus and building confidence like a muscle. I could tell him that it only makes sense that he would struggle a little and give him some activities to try. But that's not good enough. My goal is to help him see the tools he already has.

"I know you've been through this before, Chris. There must have been times when you were trying something new and your confidence was fragile. Where have you built yourself back up before? What's worked for you in the past?"

He's quiet. His eyebrows are pressed together as if trying to squeeze an idea out of his brain. Then, as if discovering his keys were hiding in his pocket the entire time, he begins to shake his head, even laugh a bit.

"Can I share a story with you?" As if he hopes I'd say no.

"Absolutely Chris, I'm super interested."

"Before I had started teaching in the Juvenile Corrections Center, before I had even graduated college, I had to work for a semester as a student teacher. My assignment was an eighth-grade geography class: maps, culture, and name that capital. In my 20-year-old mind, it was going to be a relatively easy assignment, but that's before I understood just how dangerous eighth-grade children can be, or how dedicated Carol, my mentor teacher would be."

As Chris tells the story, his body relaxes. He is connecting to the emotions of the past, a positive memory lost in the shadows of his mind and now rediscovered, providing the same warm feeling as before.

"Carol had been teaching for the better part of 30 years. While she was only a couple of years away from full retirement, she approached the job with the same professionalism and gusto I would have imagined she had when she first began instructing." He smiles as if meeting her for the first time again.

"This gusto meant I was going to have to work, and work hard. Carol would videotape my instruction and have me take it home, watch it, and write a paper on what I could improve. She would spell-check my lesson plans, she would have me show up early and leave late, she would count how many times I said "um" while figuring out what to say next, which was 25 times during one class, and she forced me to look at the profession of teaching as something we constantly improve upon, or else should not enter into in the first place. She was a professional, one of the best. I hated doing the work, but knew it was preparing me."

His chest expands. He sits upright and becomes matter-of-fact in his description.

"A few weeks into the part of my internship that had me teaching alone the majority of the day, what she'd been preparing me for became painfully clear. The class had gone sideways. The kids weren't listening. They were throwing papers, sleeping, laughing, and passing notes. I have no idea how it happened, but somewhere in that one-hour class, the kids I thought respected me and thought I was the cool teacher had suddenly created Lord of the Flies, classroom edition." He smiles as one might if watching a movie they'd seen before, seeing the danger yet knowing the hero will make it through the whole time.

"I was trying everything I could to get them in order only to have the worst possible outcome. Carol had to come back into the class to get them back in line. It was humiliating. I started to beat myself up mentally thinking maybe I wasn't cut out for teaching. That thought popped into my mind before Carol could get control of the class." He shakes his head, still embarrassed years later.

"That sounds painful." I prompt, trying to remind him to keep connecting the story to his current experience.

"Carol saw this, perhaps felt it," he continues. "She had no intention of letting those thoughts fester. She asked me how I felt. I told her I felt horrible, stupid, and unqualified. And she acknowledged the feelings. 'You're going to have those days,' she said. And, as she said this, she was sitting in her chair, behind the old brown, metal behemoth of a desk that all teachers used to own." He warms to his story as if bragging about meeting a personal hero.

"She began opening the large file drawer on the bottom right of the desk. 'You are going to have days like today, lots of them. You can just plan on that.' She looked into the contents of the overloaded file. 'When they do come, I've found they seem to create something of a mental file in our heads that, if we don't do something about, can eventually lead us to believe the exact things you are thinking about now.'" Now Chris is almost channeling her, transferring the wisdom on to me as it had been given to him.

"As she turned to show me the contents of the drawer, I noticed the notes, letters, and cards overflowing. 'These are all the messages I've gotten from kids, parents, and co-workers. There are even a few I've written to myself on days that went well. All of these precious letters tell me that, while I still may have room to improve, there are things I'm doing well right now, places I'm making a difference right now, and people I have an impact on despite the momentary feeling this rough day is generating.'" His eyes are now on fire with this formative experience brought back to life.

"That teacher said, 'There are always going to be two files you get to choose from. One that only gets filled in the challenging times that tells you that you're not good enough, unqualified, and worse. Or the one that gives you a more complete picture. The one that reminds you of all the good you have done, all the impact you have made, and how important you are to others. The only difference in these files is the simple fact that one happens outside of your control and the other, the important one, the one that allows you to make a difference, well, you have to build that one on your own.'"

"Wow," I say, too caught up in the story to come up with anything else.

"I sat there looking at all of those letters and thought to myself that there was no way I'd ever get that many pieces of encouragement as long as I lived. And that's when she gave me the final piece of advice, the part that helped me turn that very same day around. She asked, 'What do you have for your file today?'"

I'm floored by the simple beauty of the story.

"What an amazing experience, Chris. Did her advice work?"

"Yeah, it worked, almost immediately. Before the conversation, I was planning on skipping out on coaching that evening. I had volunteered to coach volleyball and planned on letting the other coach take over for the day. My day had been crap and I was cutting my losses. But, after the conversation, I went. And, during that same practice, I noticed how far along one of the players had come, and I realized that I played a part in that."

"So it's about actively building the file where you are at. That sounds easy enough. And, since it is about right now, where can we actively build this file right now? What are you currently proud about? What feels like freedom right now that you might be missing? Where are you currently having an impact?"

That mentor from his past had struck a deep nerve. What she had given Chris was a strategy for purposefully overcoming his natural tendency to identify all the places he was at

118

risk. Now he would identify where he was doing well at the same time. Purposefully building evidence.

Over the ensuing weeks, Chris and I focused on helping him purposely record those things that had gone well, that he was proud about, and that he had accomplished as they happened. I had him create lists of all the things he was currently doing that felt like freedom to him. In the course of one week, he came up with close to a hundred different activities, from taking a walk with his wife to volunteering with a local non-profit. He began to identify conversations with clients at his current business, the same conversations he had dreaded before, and even began recognizing how running made him feel again.

These were things that had been happening all along, but he hadn't been purposely paying attention to them. His brain had been spending the majority of time looking for the things that were going wrong. Initially, he'd looked the same way at his past, identifying only the threats until he looked more closely. Now, he was finding out he could do the same thing in the present.

I found many clients had similar stories. A mentor, teacher, parent, or even just a friend had helped them focus on what was going right in their lives when they needed it most. Now they were able to unleash energy or get through tough times by opening that file.

I challenged my clients to make it a formal process. Some would create actual files on their computers that kept track of what they'd done and were currently doing. They logged their accomplishments, awards, times of impact, and the times they'd felt most alive. They could access these files any time and add to them daily or weekly.

For some people, it turned into weekly conversations with friends, co-workers, and business connections. They would practice talking about what had gone well the previous week and work together to help each other refine their work. By keeping each other's brains fixed on those things that gave them confidence, they proved the validation needed to convince their brains that they were still progressing and still bringing value to the world.

Building this file, creating the tangible evidence of progress, is an essential ingredient needed for tackling big challenges, handling major change, or pushing ourselves to new levels. But, for so many, it's neglected and atrophied. It's like going to the gym. Only, instead of building biceps or hamstrings, we can build the parts of our brain that give strength to believe in ourselves.

In a short number of weeks, I could hear the change in Chris.

"I guess maybe I don't have to get a job."

"What do you mean?" I reply, trying not to make the grin on my face too noticeable.

"Well, I've been tracking what really gets me engaged, and I realize there are a lot of other things I could do. I can get a job, but I'm not going to get just any job. I'm going to do something I care about and that needs my unique talents."

"So, you're still looking for a job, right?" I ask, a bit concerned that maybe he's gone off the deep end.

"Absolutely. In a couple of months I'm no longer going to have one, so I'll need something. I think I'm just realizing that I bring a lot to the table. Maybe a job can be a place to experience freedom at a different level, and that seems to be changing how I might approach my next move."

"What do you think has changed for you?"

"Every time I look at what I did well this day or this week, it's like a little more weight falls off my back and I'm able to focus more on what else I want to do. I'm still freaked out about my current job ending, but it doesn't overwhelm me as much anymore because I know there are so many things I can do to make an impact, where I can bring value."

"What makes you think you can do this?" I'm trying to challenge him a bit and test this muscle he's developing.

"I engage people, I care about people. I go above and beyond in my work and leave things better than I found them."

"Why should I believe all of that?" Pushing a little more.

"I could show you all the things I've done in the last couple of weeks, the interactions I have with people and the outcomes I have created. I could show you my experience and expertise."

"And, if I still don't believe? If you show me all your evidence, qualifications, results, and experience, but I still don't believe you, what then?"

He pauses for a moment, initially frustrated, then with a deep breath, is calm in his response. "Then I guess I don't care. Maybe you're not the person I need to convince. Maybe I just need to find others who are ready to acknowledge that I bring a lot of value. The only person I need to believe in this whole equation is myself."

And with that simple yet remarkable statement, Chris marked the removal of dependency. He had changed the equation in his head. No longer did his security come from a job, a degree, or a company. Validation could be found doing the things he did well and the things that made him feel most alive. Now he could pull through in tough times, adjust when things changed and have confidence to communicate his value.

I should have been happy for him, happy for myself and my part in helping him along in the process. But I wasn't. The biggest danger of attempting to be real with a client is the hypocrisy. Clients can provide a mirror if you are willing to look. If you are brave enough to know you might not like what you see.

What do I know I do well? Where am I having an impact? Where am I already doing those things that I define as important to me? What do I truly believe about myself? What value do you bring and how are you already sharing it right now? It's not that I hadn't answered them before, that I didn't have a current answer, but as deep as I was asking my clients to dig, I wondered if I was answering them fully enough myself.

This was a new process for me as much as it was for them. With it came new questions. Is this something I can make a business out of? Do I really believe it or am I just going through the motions? Would people still find value in what I do if I'm not bringing them the answers?

12
RISK

"I had a conversation the other day and I'm not sure how I feel about it." Chris has a confused look on his face.

"Sounds interesting, Chris. What is it?"

"It was with a recruiter. He was calling about a job." He seems downright unexcited.

"That's a good thing, right?"

"It's a good position. The salary is excellent— more than I'm making now, with potential to make a lot more in the near future."

"Sounding even better. Not really seeing the problem here."

"When the recruiter started to explain the position to me, it almost immediately felt wrong." His eyebrows are pinched together.

"Like he was lying or some other kind of wrong?"

"Wrong like it didn't fit me, even though I met all the qualifications and it was similar to things I have done in the past."

"So, what did you do?"

"I told him I wasn't interested."

"And is that what you're wondering about?"

"It just felt like I should have explored it a bit more. Like I was supposed to at least try and get the position."

"What do you think would have happened if you would have followed through on all of this? If you went through with the interview, tried your ass off to get the job and got it?"

"That's pretty easy actually. I would have hated it. Or, at the very least, I would have gotten really bored with it."

"So what did saying no feel like?"

"It felt scary at first. Like I should be telling him that I want the job. Then it felt awesome."

"Let's break that down. Tell me about the scary part in the beginning."

"I felt like I was failing. Like this is what I was supposed to be doing and, in saying no, I was taking an opportunity off the table. My head was running through a bunch of scenarios that included not having another job opportunity in the future, being unemployed in a month or so and other worst case scenarios."

"And the excitement? Tell me about that."

"For the first time, it felt like I had a bit of control. It was like standing up for myself for the first time. Like I don't need saving anymore. I thanked him for his time. I was polite about it and yet it felt so powerful. I still question it, but, if I'm honest, I loved the feeling."

"Sounds like you took control of your own failure."

"What do you mean by that?"

"You just talked about how you could see the job being

pretty boring for you and potentially hating it. And, if you know that already, what are the chances that you end up failing? At least not succeeding like you could somewhere else?"

"Chances are pretty high."

"Then the discomfort you initially felt when you turned it down was just you being more honest with the feeling and failing at the job sooner than later."

"Failing just seems like a cruel term."

"I'm only using it because it's the term you use so often." I say, baiting him to respond.

"What are you talking about?"

"Every time you talk about your past experiences, your former business, the coaching position, and even your current job, you use the word failure.

"But those are failures." He sounds frustrated.

"If you believe that's what they are, maybe. But how are they any different than what you just described with the potential job you recently turned down?"

"It's different because the business cost me a lot of money, the coaching position was embarrassing and the current position just feels like a waste of time. Saying no to the job didn't cost me anything."

"It cost you the opportunity for that job and the income that would have come with it. But let's put that aside for a moment. I'm curious, how does this play out in your running? Was that a failure too? You damaged your Achilles and can't run anymore, maybe never again. Was all that just a waste of time?"

"Hey, that's not funny. You know I miss running horribly. Are you just trying to piss me off now?"

"Was it a waste of time?" I dig deeper.

"No, it wasn't. You know it wasn't," he shoots back immediately.

"Why?"

"Because it got me through a lot, because sometimes running felt like the only thing I was good at, because it taught me so much."

"But if you have this injury and can't do it anymore, if it's not this perfect thing for you to do forever, how was it not a mistake? Not just a waste of time?"

"I may not be able to run again, but I can assure you it was the right thing at the time."

"And how is that any different from your past jobs, and from right now?"

He pauses. Not convinced but considering.

"Losing the business and the jobs ending felt like a big waste of time. I'm supposed to be acting on my purpose, and it was obvious those jobs weren't my purpose so they felt much more like a failure."

"Was running your purpose?"

"For a while I thought so."

"And now?"

"I guess not."

"But for a time, maybe it was?"

"Yes, I think so." He sounds confused again.

"That's because you made it that way, Chris. You made it purposeful. And, because of that, you redefined failure. When you didn't finish something, you got back up and tried again. You found distances you couldn't run, and failed, and you might have put yourself in a position where you can't run anymore, the biggest failure. But you made them meaningful."

"I did? You think it was my choice?"

"How could it not be your choice? It's the same choice with everything you've been through. Your failures make you stronger because you got back up, because you choose to learn so much through them, because they give you skills, abilities, and wisdom you can take with you anywhere. In your failure, you showcase your strength."

"Yeah, I think I can see that."

"And now that you're owning it, you have the ability to create it faster. You are beginning to stand up for yourself quicker. There's the same potential of failure as before, but it's in your control now. Instead of waiting for external influences to create the failure for you, you're making it on your own and feeling the validation that comes from realizing you're going to get back up, regardless of what happens. You know it because you've done it so many times before."

"Like the recruiter and turning down the job?"

"Yes, you realized it wasn't a good fit, and that you have enough value that you don't have to depend on every opportunity in front of you. This is a big deal, Chris. You're not seeking validation externally anymore. You're starting to create it internally. Taking control of the thing you need."

"That's what felt so damn good about the call. It's what you mean by validation. As if I stood up for myself for the first time."

"The business and the other jobs only feel more like failure because you waited for someone to force you to believe in yourself because there was no other choice. You waited for the world to tell you, show you, and kick you in the stomach before you got to realize that you could take care of yourself after all. The validation you were seeking has been available the whole time."

"Wait a minute. Where did you come up with all this?

We've never talked about any of this before."

"I learned it from you, Chris. I realized you've been depending on me for your validation. Yet, the only time you really get that validation is when you create it yourself." I am being completely honest with him, vulnerable, like we have nothing to hide. "Here's what I want. I want you to go out and practice what you learned with the recruiter. Practice failing. Acknowledge your abilities. And quit relying on me."

I leave abruptly.

This shift from consultant to coach was beginning to get too uncomfortable for me. Like I was stealing his, or someone else's process. In the middle of that conversation, I realized we were very close to ending our relationship. At first, I thought I could keep going, move past the discomfort I felt in my own feeling of hypocrisy, even if I didn't know where it was coming from. But now it was painfully clear the end was in sight.

I was talking to him about his failures and not willing to confront my own at the same time. I wasn't confident enough to move forward, yet knowing full well what needed to be done.

When I stopped trying to give my clients the right solution, a tactic that now in hindsight seemed more about satisfying my own needs, they found better solutions on their own. They created new jobs, new businesses, and entirely new ways of living that would have seemed impossible 20 years ago. When their jobs stagnated, they started driving for Uber at night and working on a new business during the day. With no set path, they did contract work, wrote blogs, and found others like them. They learned to make a living talking about the things they cared about most deeply. When the traditional job no longer worked, they learned to make their living on boats, in small houses, in industries that didn't exist weeks ago and in jobs that were years ahead of their time. They stopped waiting to get on the right track and made the track they were on the right one for them.

They took their discomfort and did something about it. They used the obstacles and turned them around to make their own future. They were stronger than me.

It was remarkable to see the new confidence Chris wore. He received more calls over the next couple of weeks, all of them off the mark, and all of them great for his confidence. He said it was like a little shot in the arm every time he told someone no. It had been so long since he'd stood up for himself.

His job search was turned on its head. No longer was he trying to find a job that he could convince himself he fit into. Now he was looking for the job that fit him. He even started to consider what it would look like stepping back out on his own. He hadn't allowed himself to consider this since closing the doors on his last business.

But it wasn't enough, and I knew it. As much as it had improved from his willingness to work, his progress was slowed by my own needs. I was in the way, but I was scared, too. What if I'm holding him back from what he could be? What if he failed again?

And there it was. My own belief I might be able to save him was preventing him from seeing he truly didn't need to be saved at all. The security he was seeking wasn't mine to give him. I knew this but wasn't sure if I was comfortable with it. How could I help him fully believe in himself when I'm still doubting my own conviction?

Chris's value, my own value, was not simply about the job we did, but was about who we were. A person's self-worth is not their net worth. A title does not signify worth and potential is not confined by what happens from 9 to 5. We have to be students of our strengths, experts of our potential, and have a graduate level understanding of the value we can bring to the world. Only when we trust our value do we truly create the security we're seeking. But to believe, we have to take a risk.

***

Chris is back, and he's excited. Neither of us want to talk about my abrupt departure, so we move forward as if nothing has changed.

"Ok, I've had a number of jobs and an even bigger number of interviews I've turned down. Now, I need you to help me decide which one I should take." He doesn't make eye contact.

"Why are you coming to me for the answer?" It's a direct response meant to get his attention immediately.

"Because you've always been helpful. And I feel like I need you to point me in the right direction. The next choice is going to be pretty important professionally, and I need you to help me figure it out."

I know he is placating me, trying to make me feel better, useful. But it's having the opposite effect.

"How many times have I heard you talk about the two houses analogy?" Now I'm purposely trying to provoke him.

"I don't need some analogy right now. I need the answer."

"Say I'm going to invite you to my house, and I can give you one of two sets of directions. You tell me which one you would rather have."

"I get it," he says, trying to get me to stop.

"The first set of directions includes a list of all the countries where you won't find the house, the cities I don't live in, the streets I don't live on, the addresses that are not mine, what colors my house isn't, the dogs I don't have, and the cars you won't see in the street."

He's annoyed now, not responding. He knows full well

where I'm going with this. Most people are only good at knowing what they don't want. Consciously stating a direction is a much harder.

"Or, I can give you a set of directions that include the exact country, state, city, street and address that my house is in. I can give you GPS coordinates. I can tell you the house color, the dog that might greet you and the cars that will be parked in the driveway. Which would you like?"

"Are you done?"

"Which one have you been using? Which set of directions?"

"You were the one that told me to go out and fail. To practice saying no."

"I did. And now I'm asking you a different question."

"I don't know where I'm going. I just started to realize what was important to me. I barely started being able to see it. How do you expect me to suddenly figure out where I want to go?" Chris's face turns red with frustration.

"Stand up for yourself man!" I'm surprised with the emotion in my own response. "I can tell you all this, but eventually you're going to have to believe it for yourself. Come on! Step out! Be the creative person you know you can be. You were meant to explore the unknown, not rest comfortably in the known. You were made to create, not recreate. You're not a position in a production line, you're the magic that makes a production line possible."

I'm speaking harshly and directly, pulling no punches, trying to get him over the wall and past the protective barriers his mind has built. It's an emotion that seems to come easily right now, like it was just beneath the surface for me. I'm doing my best to make it about him.

I go on. "Who do you want to be? You've been letting other people say it for you and define it for you for too long.

Somewhere in the depth of those overwhelming voices you need to fight. They're not getting quieter so you have to get louder. You have to shout it from the rooftops. At the very least you have to say it out loud."

He looks devastated. "But I've done it before. I've had goals, only to fall short. I've had dreams and said them out loud, only to let myself and those around me down."

His words hit me right in the gut. Had I created this? I'm suddenly angry with him, with myself, the world. My voice ratchets up a notch.

"Yes, you have. You've taken some pretty big risks and felt some pretty big losses. Does that mean you quit now? You throw in the towel because you got roughed up a bit? What good is it to know your value if you're not going to do anything with it? What about creating something meaningful, something worth the pain you've gone through?"

It feels like a bad breakup, like I'm trying to get him angry enough to leave or make myself feel better by pissing him off.

"That's easy to say," Chris says. "But you don't know how it feels inside. The doubt, the fear, the questioning of the steps I'm taking all the time. I want to hear you, I do, but, honestly, I'm scared."

"I get it, Chris, I really do. I understand the disappointment of having had the rules change, of your expectations not meeting with reality, of hoping for an outcome only to have it change over and over again. I am not asking for you to be right, I'm asking you to try again. You're approaching this as if losing will cost you your life. I can assure you the only thing at risk is your lifestyle. The only things in play are your ego, your pride. Who cares about what other people think about you, that's none of your business to begin with anyway."

He doesn't respond. He's letting the information sink in and fighting an internal battle.

"If no one's giving you your value anymore, you have to go out and create it on your own. And it starts with defining it on your own. It's okay to be wrong, Chris. It's not okay to wait anymore. You don't need to wait for someone else, for another job, for the right time, or for someone else to give you permission. You need to put your goddamn stake in the ground—"

And then Chris interrupts me. "Look. I want to free people from the traps they create in their minds. To help them break free from the stories that other people have put in their heads about what they are supposed to do or who they are supposed to be. I want them to know freedom and I want that to be my job, whatever it looks like. I need it to be what I do, because it's what I was meant to do."

His eyes fill with tears. His chin quivering, he looks directly at me with the determination of a soldier and the vulnerability of a man exposed.

"I have no idea how I'm going to do this."

"Trust your value, Chris. You've got all the tools you need."

"I'm not sure I even know what that means."

"Do you believe you can do it?"

"Yes."

"Then you don't need me anymore."

I turned, and without looking back, I left Chris for the last time.

13
TRUST

The heart of the Educo philosophy is a question: What more is available? It's about pulling out the potential, an unrelenting focus on what is possible creating the belief that more is always available. There are hundreds of ways to ask the same question, and all of us are searching for a better question whether we know it or not. Chris was fully committed to his own question now.

To extract from. The right question pulls out what's inside, reveals it to the world, and more importantly to the individual.

Children think like this. They move for hours on end driven by curiosity. They follow the obsession of a single inquiry for days and ask questions from every angle, filled with the motivation only wonder can create. As we get older, this potential for natural engagement doesn't leave us. We leave it, instead.

What does it look like? Where do you see it happening? What are the possibilities? How could this be unique to you? Questions that can keep the same child-like motivation at any age.

The right questions hold the keys to sustainable motivation. They call us to explore our potential and answer the underlying "what if" that lies within each of us. Ironically, I'd spent so much time trying to get Chris focused on a question that would inspire him recently that I wasn't prepared for him to progress so fast. I knew from the beginning he was going to need someone more qualified than me to get him to the next level. By the time I left, we were both aware of this limitation.

When we started this thing, it was just an idea, him speaking and me helping him as a consultant. I had a graduate degree and a background helping individuals and small companies achieve goals. Doing this wasn't my full-time job, but I loved it, and I knew how to make it practical for people. It was supposed to be a fun exploration with Chris, but something had gotten both of us frightened early on. Afraid of an idea that was bigger than either of us had experienced before, we quickly stepped the idea back, not knowing this would begin the process that would eventually lead to such an utter breakdown.

Things just seemed to build on themselves. The momentum of the decisions we were making seemed to take over. His attempts at finding validation and security, my shortsighted recommendations, chasing a dream of achievement defined by someone else, outcomes out of our control, the goals he was supposed to achieve.

When I look back at that time, I realize in some ways it had been strangely comforting to see Chris go through his struggles. It meant he still needed me. I got to be his hero, the one who saved the day, sometimes simply the one who kept him off the ledge. I was protecting him.

I was a problem-solver. An expert trained in a school of thought that convinces ourselves that we have the solution for someone else's problem. People from this school are great at offering the seven best strategies, the five keys to success, the three things you need to do to become a millionaire, and every other guaranteed method to solving your problem without identifying what you really want in the first place. It's a great business model, because it requires an external solution, it makes me indispensable, and the client, dependent.

Chris didn't need a new bridge. He needed to cross the one he had already built. He didn't need my solution, he needed to understand he was the solution. Instead of completely re-inventing ourselves every time we look for a new goal, we should be using what we have already. Then we can focus energy on the small bits that need adjustment instead of fearfully trying to change our entire being. I knew this now.

Ultimately, the breakdown was a blessing. Chris forcing me to change my style and, little by little, him changing his own direction. Knowing what was important to him, what he wanted to create, this undefined yet clearly visible idea of freedom, had shifted his focus from what he could achieve to what he could deliver. Something completely within his control.

We had built back his confidence, together. I knew this and was proud of what we had done. His process, define what is important, track validation, build the file, build the confidence, it had all worked so well. And it was easy for me to follow.

He had gone from trying to be good at being someone else to learning how to be himself. Having that puzzle to solve would set in motion an electrochemical process in the brain that brought wonder and excitement. He was exciting to watch, and I had no idea just how far he could go.

What's possible? Where could I go from here? These were the questions I knew would keep him engaged.

But his future was beyond my capabilities. You can't take someone further that you have been yourself. Someone told me that once. I don't remember who, but I think they have a point. It's sound advice I need to follow, for Chris's sake.

I'd been isolated in my office for weeks trying to figure out what to do next.

I was trying to find another coach that might be able to help Chris get to the next level. I was also trying to figure out how to help him make the transition to a better coach instead of continuing to work with me and risk stagnating again.

I wasn't prepared when Chris walked in. I hadn't expected to see him so soon. We didn't have an appointment, and he didn't ask if I had time available. He just walked directly into my office and looked me in the eye.

"We have to continue working together." He is direct and confrontational.

"What are you doing here?" I am on caught off guard.

"I'm here to demand that you start working with me again." He is even more direct.

"But you don't need me. How far you've come. From here I would only hold you back," I say feebly.

"What are you talking about?"

"Chris, we both know I'm really just winging it with this approach. Sure, we've had some success recently, but you need someone better, someone that knows what they are doing, someone more proven." I am trying to let him down easy.

He doesn't flinch. "Do you hear what you are saying? You want me to find someone else? Maybe someone that will prove my security for me? Is that what you mean?"

"No, I just mean someone more, well, no, that's not what I mean." I'm not prepared, the words aren't what I wanted them to be, this isn't what I meant, I am sure of it.

"It sounds like you are trying to tell me I need to find security in someone else again. You and I both know that won't work." His gaze is focused, as if looking through me.

"But I'm the one that took you down the wrong path in the first place." I have to remind him of my limitations. I have to protect him.

"I don't blame you for how things turned out at first. For you being so focused on trying to help me find jobs, and strategies that would give me a sense of security, it's what I was asking for at the time. Now what I really need is for you to help me believe that I can do the things I need to keep this feeling we have created together. I need more of that, not less. I need just as much help developing security and validation internally as I did finding them externally. I trust you, more than anyone else, to help me continue to do that."

His delivery, amazing. If he could only see his confidence right now.

"How do you know we can keep doing that in the future? How can you be so sure?" I try again to deflect it back on him.

He smiles like he's telling me something that should be obvious to both of us. "Like everything else, we've done this before."

"When have we done it before?" I shake my head.

"Don't you remember helping me when I was running? Whenever I started to think I couldn't do it anymore, you were there to tell me that I was going to be okay and to keep moving. It was just the security I needed at the time. When I doubted my reasons for even signing up for the race, you reminded me that I was doing it for fun. I remember, because it was the exact validation I was looking for at the time."

"I remember," I say gratefully. "And I must say, it means a lot to me that you do too. I'm impressed that you found value in those interactions when I wasn't sure if you heard me in the first place. I didn't know." I try to hide the excitement I feel for his recognition.

"It's something you can do so well when you want, and I'm going to need it in the future." he says. "Somewhere along the way, I think we both got convinced that what I needed was for you to protect me against all the externalities. Like you could shield me from the changes in the market, from companies being bought or sold, from business needs shifting at a moment's notice, or these other things out of our control."

"Ok, Chris. Maybe we can create security together, but I've been so focused on getting validation through predictable avenues for so long I'm not sure I'll be of much use. Where you are going there are no maps, no defined ways to measure success, how will we even know if I'm helping or not?"

"You really think I'll never need external validation anymore? You think I won't still want acknowledgment from other people, from other companies, from the market itself?" He sounds so sure of himself.

"I suppose you probably will." I'm starting to cave.

"And do you believe, because I'm doing a better job at creating my own sense of security, that I won't want to still have it reinforced from the outside? That I won't want better contracts, companies that I trust or a job I don't have to worry about leaving every other day?"

"Well, I guess if you look at it from that angle, I see what you mean. But if those things aren't going away, how do we make sure we don't get distracted by them again?"

"By focusing on the things we do control. The reasons I want to do all this stuff in the first place. By getting better at understanding what I do well and leveraging successes I've had in the past. And by remaining hyper vigilant in those areas where I've been improving. I want create freedom every single day. I'm committed to act on all the insight we've had.

Now I need you to help me trust it. Will you?"

There it was. He wanted me to trust him when the entire time I had expected—at times even demanded—his trust in me. I felt cornered, like I had nowhere else to hide, like I'd been found out, finally exposed for my biggest shortcoming.

"You don't know what you're asking, Chris."

"You know exactly what I'm asking. And I know why you're trying to run away."

"What do you think you know?"

"I know you are afraid. I know the idea of your own potential scares the hell out of you. I know that, deep down, you know more is available but you are too tied to the same old idea of security. I know you are petrified of losing something you've never fully had, something you stay awake at night worrying you will never achieve, and, ultimately, something you don't believe you deserve."

"What is that?"

"To feel as though you truly have value. That you just might be worth the effort, that you have something to bring to the world and you don't need to be fixed. That the world needs what you have to deliver. Your potential, our potential, is only available fully if we are brave enough to risk, vulnerable enough to be honest, courageous enough to trust ourselves. I'm asking you to trust me."

"I'll have to think about it, Chris." I leave the room quickly, one last attempt to get away.

I don't know what else to say. He hit me with all of it at once. In response, I feel the pull of my brain against itself. My executive system wants to give reasoned thoughts, to think through things and reasonably plan my next move. My limbic system wants to retreat, to react, to defend and shut off for protection. It's like two separate people are wrestling over the real me.

So long I've been convinced I had to choose between my rational side and the dreamer in me. I've put my desires aside for the realities of life. But what if both sides could work together?

For a moment, as I stand there battling with myself, I see the possibility of a future where people make understanding their unique value a priority, where they are able to realize their potential, where we begin to trust our ability to create a better future again. One where we believe in our ability to solve problems we haven't even recognized. Where the future is a creation of our own design, not just one we are reacting to. One in which we know that more is always available if we are willing to work to find it. Starting with ourselves.

Chris is asking me to move forward. He is inviting me to step out into the unknown, and committing to do the same himself. I can see he's always been ready. Now his courage outshines mine.

"Trust your value." Was that his voice, or was it mine?

I stand at the mirror in my office, taking a deep and honest look at myself. Suddenly, there he is.

"Where did you come from?"

"I've been here the entire time."

"I guess I knew that."

"Are you ready?" he asks.

"To give you an answer?"

"No, you gave me the answer long ago."

"I suppose I did."

"I just want to know if you are ready to get started."

"You know I'm going to screw up."

"We both will. But that's okay. I think it's what acceptance is all about."

"I trust you," I say. "You know, I don't think I ever said that."

"But you did just now. More than that, you've been telling me that with every question you've asked. Educo, remember? It only works if you believe there's something to extract."

It's like looking in the mirror. Sometimes it takes a while to finally like what you see. To believe that person looking at you has something to offer. To trust the eyes staring back at you, knowing they see right through to the real you.

Chris smiles at me and I see my own face smiling back. And, perhaps for the first time, I see myself fully.

14
DELIVERING VALUE

So I'm working on it—this whole trust thing.

Now that Chris and I are finally one, instead of pushing back the voice, I take the chance on letting it lead the way as often as I can. Like today, getting ready to go on stage, with nearly 1,000 people waiting for me to give the opening speech for their conference.

When they asked me, I could think of one hundred reasons to say no, but none were stronger than the one reason to say yes. It's a talk about the changing economy, changes in work, but mostly it's about the urgent necessity for us to be able to trust ourselves, others and the potential found within both to create a better future.

I've had the good fortune of finding a job that allows me to speak to groups, talk about what they really want in life, and to continue working on my own. It seems that the new economy creates loads of new working options.

Things haven't always been easy street though. Old habits are hard to break. I find myself going back into protection mode when things get tough. I catch myself doubting my abilities, questioning even my own sanity still. But I know these are just momentary. I can be pretty good at getting back up, so I focus on that.

There was no line to cross or single day that everything clicked. It still feels like a constant expedition, like venturing into unknown territory and discovering great things along the way. There is no longer a finish line, just deeper pursuit. Not about what I can achieve as much as what I can deliver. And yet the achievements seem to follow.

This struggle is inherent in everyone. Part of us believes in our potential, and another side seems to be continually in protective mode. Just know that both are important parts of us.

Are we spending our time trying to have someone else create the security that we can create ourselves? Are we willing to listen to the part of ourselves that believes in our potential? What would be available if we did?

The most insistent voices we battle aren't other people trying to lead us the wrong direction. It's our own voice, doubting our abilities, that becomes so overwhelming. The part of us that is afraid of what might happen if we were to risk believing in ourselves.

Maybe every modern human is meant to be an explorer. Maybe our focus on external security and validation created the opportunity to explore in a manner that simply wasn't available before. As a species on this planet, there may be few new lands to explore, but there are unlimited depths of understanding yet to be had. We have finite places to discover on the outside but unlimited avenues to continue looking on the inside.

If we try and fail today, we just lose money or take a shot to the ego. Doing it a hundred years ago might have put us in jeopardy for life. The responsibility in this gift is simply to use it, to keep demanding something more fulfilling.

These days, I'm handling my clients differently. I'm encouraging them to be more of, well, themselves. I'm telling them they don't need to spend their time trying to be someone else. There's so much more potential in maximizing the value they already bring to the table. I'm telling them, let's stop living half-lives. No more bringing half of us to our jobs, our homes or ourselves. No more trying to be two different people in one body. Let's accept ourselves fully, because the challenges, hardships, and opportunities of the future will require us showing up 100 percent.

If we're willing to set aside the need for someone else to provide the directions for us, we can find levels of confidence, engagement, and fulfillment beyond any dream. There is no single person like us in the world, and we don't have to spend all of our time trying to be someone else. We simply have to learn to be confident in ourselves and trust our own voice. We need to believe in ourselves and teach others to do the same.

Let's use these uncertain times to ask better questions. What can we learn? What is possible? What walls can we break down? In doing this, we might just find the uncertainty is our chance to create something better for our future. The opportunities are endless if we change where we search. Success need not be tied to some external reward as much as the internal understanding of our true potential.

If we're willing to trust the value that resides within, and to explore the depths of the internal instead of the distractions of the external, we might just find everything we need right in front of us.

***

Following the talk, the company's CEO comes up to talk to me. She loved the message. She talks enthusiastically about finding ways to help her employees realize their potential, and nervously about the changing economy. She even talks about struggling with trusting her own value.

It was an amazing and humbling conversation for me. Someone who seemed to have it all together was battling the same thing as everyone else. She wanted to know what was possible.

Maybe this is what the farmer was asking about the entire time. I wonder if I still have his card?

Maybe it's what we're all asking.

I decide to engage her. Nervous at first, but excited. I can see it in her, that potential, and I know I just have to bring it out.

Educo. It's available because I believe she has value.

I know, because I trust my own.

ABOUT THE AUTHOR

Brian Fretwell is a speaker, consultant and founder of Why We Win. For 15 years, he has put people and companies in the driver's seat again. He is a captivating speaker and an unrelenting, often irreverent coach. He believes every single person should realize the value they can deliver. He lives with his wife, Jamie, and dog, Hank, in Boise, Idaho.

You can find him at www.brianfretwell.com or on LinkedIn at https://www.linkedin.com/in/bfretwell/

ACKNOWLEDGMENTS

To believe that we do anything by ourselves is a lonely proposition. Even in the doldrums of what seems like isolated, individual work, the effects of the tribe are omnipresent. The voices we surround ourselves with can help to fill in the void between doubt and confidence, often bridging the gap between idea and finished product. I have been blessed with too many of these voices to count. People that were a part of this finished directly, indirectly, and at times, without even their knowledge. This is a short list. I hope to not forget anyone.

First and foremost, my wife Jamie. For reading more drafts than would be required for punishment in a literary prison camp. To my family, who support me even when I'm not around.

To Ken Carroll for all the years of teaching me that we are always both coach and client.

To David Kilmer, the Captain. Thank you for challenging me to do something that is likely still above my pay grade as a writer. Our conversations not only helped to bring this together as a coherent story, but helped me clarify, and get to the heart of, ideas that have been in my head for years. As a great captain, you helped guide me through these turbulent waters with a focus on the benefit of rough seas as much, if not more, than the destination itself.

Mathew Cook for putting up with constant revisions yet still working tirelessly to create a book cover, Renee Settle for helping me see the book from a different perspective and opening my eyes to how we can positively affect more people through that lens. David Avrin, for pushing me to think bigger about both the book and the concept itself. Kibbee Walton for the awesome headshot and for being a constant source of inspiration.

To all of my friends who have been tired of hearing me say "I'm writing a book" for too many years. I appreciate all the support, encouragement and even the frank discussions about not being a perfectionist and getting the damn thing done.

All of the pre-readers. Kibbee Walton, Tom Moore, Jon Totten, Celestina Amor Settle, Jillana Finnegan, Sara Moore, Brian Herman, Allison Dunn, Charlie Vogel, and anyone else I might have missed. The feedback was invaluable and helped to both shape the final product and give me the confidence that perhaps more than ten people will read the book. You gave your time and your honest feedback, both are commodities in short supply. I appreciate all your input more than you might know.

And, to anyone who was a part of this, or simply took the time to read the book, I am both humbled and honored that you would want to be a part of the process. Thank you for being a part of this journey, and for letting me be a part of yours.